Altered States of Consciousness

Altered States of Consciousness

Developing Psychic Abilities

Madonna F. Merced, Psychic Medium

iUniverse, Inc.
New York Lincoln Shanghai

Altered States of Consciousness
Developing Psychic Abilities

iUniverse books may be ordered through booksellers or by contacting:

iUniverse
2021 Pine Lake Road, Suite 100
Lincoln, NE 68512
www.iuniverse.com
1-800-Authors (1-800-288-4677)

ISBN-13: 978-0-595-35906-6 (pbk)
ISBN-13: 978-0-595-80361-3 (ebk)
ISBN-10: 0-595-35906-X (pbk)
ISBN-10: 0-595-80361-X (ebk)

Printed in the United States of America

I dedicate this book to my husband, Victor Merced, who has always encouraged me to pursue my dreams. Together, accompanied by a host of guardian angels, we have journeyed along this path I have chosen in life with confidence.

CONTENTS

ACKNOWLEDGMENTS

My guardian angels and spirit guides who direct my path.

My parents, now both deceased, Vernon and Helen, for raising me in an open-minded environment filled with love.

To my sisters Helen and Neva and my nephew Jacob, thank you for the encouragement.

As always, thanks to my dear friends, Claudia and Maria, who have encouraged me to follow my heart.

Special thanks to Anabel Cazares, Woodburn, Oregon, who provided the Author's photograph.

How we perceive time and space determines our particular state of consciousness or reality. Everyday, life seems to demand we create and place parameters around things as well as events in our life. This need provides a road map for most experiences we may encounter, but it also inhibits our ability to see the world differently. When you expand your realm of reality through the development of your psychic ability, your conscious awareness, you will see it is quite possible to abandon or modify self-limiting concepts created by the mind.

Madonna F. Merced, Psychic Medium

Preface

Psychic Abilities

Over the years, I have worked with many clients. Most expressed an interest in learning how to acquire psychic abilities. My goal in writing this book is to provide a practical guide on developing psychic abilities to those who are interested in learning the techniques. What you will quickly come to understand is that time and consistency are essential ingredients to your success. While your interests may vary in how you want to use your skills, learning even the basic practices can certainly help you attain a more positive approach to interacting with people and achieving life goals.

I have outlined a systematic process that will facilitate your learning by building on each practice you successfully complete. Attaining proficiency of each practice will depend on the amount of time you commit to each learning session and your ability to focus. Mastery of any endeavor requires understanding what it will take to achieve success, focus, commitment, and repetition. As you feel comfortable in what you have learned during the practices, your ability to concentrate and comprehend the skill will become greater.

Subsequently, I will describe my own beliefs about the soul's journey through the physical world. However, for now, I want to mention that I believe each of us is born into the physical world with a mission to complete. If this mission includes developing your psychic gift, you will discover the information that is necessary to achieve that goal. Regardless of how you may intend to use your ability at the beginning of your study, when the right moment arrives during your practices and you ask the question, you will be directed on what to do next.

To everyone who is interested in a straightforward approach to developing your psychic abilities, this book is for you.

CHAPTER 1

Introduction

Human beings are complex. Height and weight define our dimensional bodies. To exist, we eat organic foodstuffs, drink water, and breathe air. In order to express ourselves outwardly, aside from the use of language, we utilize our arms, hands, legs, feet, ears, eyes, and head, which require us to employ the brain. Some body reactions are naturally programmed responses, such as breathing. On the other hand, in other actions, we want the body to take requires us to think about what we want to do and then prompt our physical appendages to act accordingly. Depending on what we tell it to do, the mind has the capacity to create a masterpiece or a disaster.

Most often, our psychic capability lies dormant and may never be tapped, given that we have access to sophisticated communication devices. However, if developed, the skill can be a powerful tool and can assist the everyday person to achieve many things, including helping others. For this reason, I suggest, before anyone embarks upon the endeavor to awaken or enhance his or her natural psychic gift, he or she take the time to acquire an understanding of what this power ultimately means.

As with most things in life, psychic power is described in many ways. In the past, it has been viewed as a gift that only a few chosen individuals could access. In general, this extraordinary competency is diverse by nature. During their life, on some level, most people experience the phenomena. Whether it is a mother overwhelmed by the feeling her child is in danger or a partner sensing a significant other needs him or her, in each instance, I am certain it involves a psychic connection. Coincidence usually involves a more complex interaction with the intelligent universe and our subconscious than can be understood by those who have not pursued the development their deep psychic awareness.

Altered state, telepathy, astral travel, psychometric ability, clairvoyance, and channeling can all be part of the psychic experience. Each unique spiritual encounter you will have can create the possibility for your subconscious to interact differently with the intelligent universe. Appreciating these encounters and viewing them in a positive manner will be valuable to your overall psychic development. Each experience will assist you in becoming increasingly more comfortable with your ability. By definition, even though some of the experiences you might have could be described as mystical, this does not mean you are interacting or communing with dark energy. The more you come to understand the process, the easier it will become to let go of any stereotypes you may have regarding what a psychic is or is not. In our culture, the psychic art has been associated with magical arts involving the darker connection to the other side or spiritual realm. Often feared, those who did engage in such activities were thought to be committing sacrilegious acts against God. Each time I go into a group to do a reading, some individuals want to be reassured about who I am in contact with on the other side. They will inevitably want to know if the church condones my activities. I take every opportunity to describe how I communicate with spirits and what I do to prepare. This discussion is also coupled with my own personal spiritual beliefs. Even after a detailed review of my process and beliefs, the majority of individuals I work with still believe there is something dark about the profession. My hope for those individuals who read this book is that they will come to understand the psychic realm and realize how natural it is for everyone to pursue the experience.

My intent is to provide you with the basic steps needed to develop your abilities. I believe that not everyone is intended to fully develop his or her psychic abilities. However, as you complete each practice and learn the basic psychic drills provided in the book, you will have a sufficient amount of knowledge to experience your psychic power. For those with an innate ability, the practices will reinforce what they already know and perhaps affirm their gift is real. Discipline and focus are key factors in developing psychic skills. The individual who decides to pursue this path, if he or she intends to master the art, should be prepared to commit the time it will require to do so correctly.

Once your journey begins and you find yourself able to use your skill, do it with the intent of not only helping yourself, but those around you. In addition, consider your psychic ability a gift that is not to be used for theatrical endeavors or in a way that mocks the profession. Remember, if you do not use the power correctly, that is, by allowing your ego to drive your decisions, it can easily disappear, never to be reawakened. Deciding what to do with your capability is a matter of choice. Moreover, once you have it, the gift is yours unless it is abused.

The term "psychic" implies, by accessing this extraordinary faculty, an individual can gain entry into a world full of information not available to the majority. As you learn more about this gift, you will see it not only includes gaining access to information. It also includes, accessing power coming from the other side, including our guardian angels, other spirits, and a universal intelligence. As you will come to discover, the brain, which is our storage unit or hard drive, has an incredible capacity for remembering. However, it must be trained. The brain will unfortunately pass on with the body. On the other hand, our mind or essence survives to live throughout eternity. The essence, of which we are, the mind, is the conduit between us and other universal intelligences or consciousnesses.

The quintessence of who we are, our mind or soul, has the ability to link with the higher intelligence. As you learn how to access this ability through the practices, you will develop an understanding of how to move into a state where the mind utilizes certain frequencies to focus on psychic functions. Coming to recognize intuition and psychic messages in addition to understanding the sixth sense will be an outcome of practicing the exercises.

When mastered, each of the following practices can be used to create a positive impact on those around you and the environment in which you live. Choosing to use your ability professionally may or may not be what you are seeking by learning to use your gift. What you will learn can potentially be used to set goals and help design a new lifestyle for you. The information will provide you with the tools to systematically and succinctly change your path. At issue here is accepting the fact we are responsible for altering our life pattern. If you listen carefully to your internal messaging, you will be able to sense when a decision is wrong for you and you need to go in a different direction. In certain situations, regardless of what you try to do, if it is part of the bigger plan you must accomplish, you will experience whatever it is you try to alter or avoid. Fortunately, if you are listening to that internal message, you will already know what you must do.

Before you begin the practices, take some time to think about your life. Go back to your childhood days, and think about how you interacted with the world. As you remember family, school, peers, and sports activities, look for themes that have reoccurred since childhood. When I look back, I see I was constantly drawn into situations in which the other side was communicating with me directly and I was always presented with opportunities to use my gift. Obviously, I was predestined to use my gift to benefit others who had lost loved ones. The point I am trying to make is that certain themes come up repeatedly during our life because we have the opportunity to recognize something that needs to be changed or implement some piece of the puzzle associated with the mission we came to accomplish during this life.

In the end, while it is possible to create a different life pattern or theme, whatever you do must be in-line with the mission you came to fulfill when born into the physical world. I cannot stress this enough. Please be aware that many of you may complete this process successful. Others will make it halfway; some will simply not succeed. During this process of learning, in due course, you will seek guidance from your guardians on the other side. You can then determine how your skill can be used or if you will pursue your training further. You will develop an understanding about being successful in any endeavor you pursue and how achieving a desired result is linked to something larger than we are.

You are an integral part of a much bigger picture. Your presence in this world, as well as on the other side, is important. By virtue of the very fact you were born, you can rest assured you came with a mission that will have an impact on someone or something. I want you to know that your attendance in this world is significant. In some way, you have improved or will enrich the existence of others.

When you read each practice and learn how to access your gift, know that my hope for you on this journey is to experience an awakening, however large or small. Gaining the knowledge to grasp your basic psychic ability can provide you with the jolt needed to alert you to your mission in life or help create the outcome you came to achieve. The awakening, if intended to occur, could stimulate you in such a way to design a life plan that enhances your life or the life of others. It does not matter who you currently are or think you are. If you want to move forward in your life, learning to access your psychic self will help you to do so.

When the universe nudged me toward my life mission as a medium, I was presented with everything I needed to make this happen. I had used my natural psychic ability throughout my life, and I had never received any formal training. However, I was blessed to have been raised in an environment in which most of my family was gifted. No one questioned my experiences with the spiritual realm. Later on in life, as the other side directed me to literature on communicating with spirits and other individuals who had psychic abilities, I realized my gift was not odd. I had always used my gift naturally, and everything I started reading affirmed that how spirits communicated through me was quite normal.

You are about to enter the world of altered states of consciousness associated with psychic activity. Take the time to develop an understanding about yourself, who you are, what patterns you have developed in life, and the direction in which you want to take the experience. Then relax. Enjoy this opportunity to discover yourself on a new level.

Chapter 2

The Altered State and Developing Our Five Senses

The act of altering a state of mind or consciousness involves practice. There are several ways to achieve this, including meditation, relaxation exercises, hypnosis, and prayer. Regardless of what you choose to call the method you use to reach an altered state, the secret to mastering any technique is practice. If you do not make the commitment to complete each practice daily until you have accomplished the outcome each requires, then you may not achieve success in developing your skills. Everyone is born with the ability to access his or her psychic ability. Daily, without any thought, most of us spontaneously experience an altered state. Over the course of your learning through the practices in the book, I will provide you with the information to achieve this state purposefully and direct your path in life to achieve the goals you desire. An important step you will take initially is developing the ability to control your mind and free yourself from the interferences you experience daily that inhibit your ability to communicate with the intelligent universe. After you are able to focus your thoughts, you will move on to some basic programming that will allow you to achieve a basic psychic level.

Acquainting yourself with the nature of this gift and how it can help you in accomplishing your goals in life will be empowering. Whether you intend to use this new skill as a tool to communicate with the spiritual realm, explore other places or dimensions, or redirect your life, what you learn and put into practice can help you to achieve success. The mind has the ability to control the body in remarkable and unused ways. Health, happiness, and success in life can all be influenced by the information you provide your mind. As you discover what creating and implementing a vision of something you want to achieve entails, whether it is buying a new car, losing weight, or becoming a practicing psychic, you will see how the process involves not only the physical body, but the material world and your senses as well. Whatever image we create, our brain will store the message. If we have programmed the message correctly, the subconscious will then use that information to assist us in doing what needs to be done in order to implement that dream or goal.

To develop the ability to program messages for your mind, you must first acquaint yourself differently with your senses, specifically hearing, touch, smell, and taste. You know the eyes allow you to see what exists in your surroundings. Your ears allow you to hear. Your hands and skin allow you to feel things. The nose allows you to smell. Finally, your taste buds allow you to taste food as well as other matter. A vital factor in creating your vision will involve recording the information from your senses in a conscientious, systematic manner that will heighten the mind's ability to facilitate intuition or the psychic sense. When you record information experienced by your senses in the brain, it will be essential to consider each sensation carefully and appreciate what is involved.

Each of us uses our senses on a daily basis just to function in the world. Yet, most people do not develop these senses to support their psychic nature. The bottom line is that our need to amplify the senses has decreased with the advent of technology, which provides numerous other avenues for communicating with others as well as assisting us in the act of everyday living. We no longer sleep in caves or in the outdoors where the only lighting available is from a campfire. Consequently, our need to smell predators or develop a keen sense of sight in order to help us identify what is hidden from normal view is no longer crucial to our survival. In the world today, the predators are different. We are required to think about the criminal profile so that we do not become a victim of crime. Furthermore, scouting for food simply involves selecting the freshest, prepackaged meat from a cold case at the local supermarket. We no longer need to stock and kill our dinner.

During the initial phase of learning how to increase your psychic awareness, you will be provided with the knowledge on how to awaken your dormant sensitivity to your internal and external world. The first stage of increasing psychic awareness requires your full participation in both worlds. Once again, completing each practice that is outlined for you daily will assist you in developing the necessary skill sets to utilize your psychic ability. Honing your awareness and senses must become a part of who you are and how you function within the environment. While your practices will initially feel structured, this feeling will subside with determination and successful completion of each. Practicing each phase of the art must become routine so that you use your skills naturally.

Our eyes capture the images for the mind to interrupt. As a psychic working with the world, you will need to sharpen your ability to see what may only be a flash. Try to imagine yourself walking in slow motion through a crowd. Record what you see. You will probably see new people you did not see when you were keeping pace with everyone. You might even see those who really are not living in this world or the flash letting you know they are here. We each have two kinds of seeing. The first type of seeing is literal, that is, you see the chair across from you, the rug on the floor, and the neighbor in his or her yard raking the leaves all captured and stored inside the mind. The second type of seeing involves seeing that which is outside of an existing reality that can be touched. It also involves scenes, images, beings and apparitions, or ghosts. One type of seeing involves quick movement and really does not necessarily take into account that which blends with the environment. The other type of seeing requires you to focus attention on your entire environment as you scan it slowly for that which is hidden from view or moving so quickly that it is difficult to see.

As a psychic medium, I can see images that most people do not. I have seen apparitions, spiritual entities in movement, and other types of manifestations that go undetected. I have also felt their physical touch as they have brushed against my hand and legs. I am highly sensitive to their presence, including severe drops in temperature both in the summer and winter, their external attempts at communication (for example, turning electronics off and on), and various other methods they use to get my attention (for example, lights flickering for no reason). I also see images in my head; hear words, letters, and names; and get messages involving movies or books all designed to identify the spirit and get my attention.

I have had multiple experiences throughout my life with psychic sight. Each time an experience has occurred, I recognized something greater than me was at work and the challenge was always to listen for the message.

A recent incident involved individuals who occupied a property owned by my husband and me. The summer had just started, and we were anxious to begin a planned holiday. Each time we had rented our second home, I had sensed a positive result with the applicant chosen to lease the property. However, for some time, I had felt the need to sell the property and move on. When the next-to-last tenant moved out, my husband and I decided to lease the home one more time. The screening process was slow until a young man showed up with the proper references. He presented his situation as urgent, saying he was starting a new job and needed to relocate his family from out of state. When I saw the young man for the first time, the sign "eviction" flashed in my mind. Concerned about the message I was receiving, I asked the screener I had hired to rethink her choice about renting to this young man and let me know if we should reconsider his application. The next day, I received a call from the screener. The young man's references had checked out, and he had the necessary financing to take possession of the property. Upon meeting with the screener and the young man, when he handed me the check, I saw red flashing in my mind and the message saying "late fees." Once again, a sign saying "eviction" flashed in my mind. Anxious to move forward and begin my summer vacation, I reluctantly entered into a lease agreement that would prove to be disastrous. Systematically, almost immediately after I accepted the lease, I started to have premonitions of issues relating to the house I had just leased, including a faulty garage door opener, the refrigerator needing replacement, flooding, and several other unpleasant activities. All of which started occurring after I returned from vacation.

Finally, after several months had passed, my husband and I decided to sell the property after the lease expired. I sensed it was time to move forward and let go of this part of our life. The following month, I received a call from the young man. He stated he needed to purchase a new car and asked for a reference. I agreed to the reference and realized I would not receive a payment for the rent. My sense (or mind's eye) showed me a zero-balance account, and I was urged to deposit funds to cover expenses for the mortgage. That night, the young man came to me in a dream. He stated his name and said he would not be making the monthly payment on the lease. Even though I was receiving clear information about what was occurring with the property, I decided to take the annual summer vacation. When I returned, I discovered the young man had not deposited the money for the lease. When I contacted the young man, he acted out in an angry, aggressive fashion. He advised me I would need to evict him if I wanted him to leave the property. The process for regaining possession of the property was less than pleasant. I had foreseen the entire incident one year in advance. My mind's eye had alerted me on a monthly basis, after leasing to the young man, that the situation was unstable. After all was said and done, we sold the property. Later, I was drawn to a real estate brochure where I found a property that we purchased in the area where my husband and I hope to relocate.

I have had many experiences in my life resembling the one I described. Most often, I listen and respond to the message.

In these situations, the outcome is positive. However, when I choose not to act on the information and warnings I receive, I suffer the consequences from my non-action. There are times when I am in a hurry and do not respond to the message I am receiving from the higher intelligence. Each of us is busy leading our lives. When we have intuitive feelings about something in our lives, we do not slow down and ponder what the message means. Learning to listen affectively to messages that come through is important. While I always gain insight from the problems I experience when I have received extensive warnings about a potential problem I could avoid, it seems senseless to burden oneself with the headache if it is not necessary.

The following practice will take place just before going to bed and involves developing your mind sight. Because this is your first practice, you will need to do several things before beginning. Select a space where you will not be bothered and can claim for your own. You will need to disconnect the telephone and any other devices that will interrupt your train of thought. If you enjoy incense, select a fragrance you enjoy, and light it before you relax. Remember, it is to your advantage to release all the information from the day's activities that cause your mind to stray. Allow yourself to get comfortable. Close your eyes. Say to your subconscious, "I am ready to begin my practice." Now open your eyes. This will allow you to give your full attention to the practices. When you are ready, begin the first practice.

Practice #1: Developing the Mind's Sight

➢ In preparing for bed, take a few minutes to look around the room where you will be sleeping. Observe where everything (furniture, clothing, clothing, and so forth) is located, what it looks like, and where it is placed. After you turn out the lights, in your mind, remember the room, and visualize where everything was located. Re-create the entire room with your eyes closed, and see yourself walking through the room with ease. As you progress in this exercise, make a mental note of each room in your house. Make a mental note of what is located in your garden outside of your home, the neighbor's garden, and so forth. As you practice these mental calisthenics, begin to realize that it becomes easier and easier. Repeat this practice each night for at least one week before moving on to the next phase.

➤ After you are comfortable with your ability to visualize various spaces and areas in your environment, you will add another step to the process. When observing the room before going to bed, look at the different colors, shapes, and textures of every object you are seeing. Close your eyes, and visualize the room. Begin to see the objects. Touch each systematically, saying to yourself as you touch each item, "I can identify this item in the light and in the dark." When you have completed the practice, open your eyes. Then relax.

➤ Start each day by taking notes with your mind everywhere you go so that you can recall your surroundings. When it is possible, examine each object you encounter. If you cannot touch it, imagine how it must feel, the texture, temperature, and so forth.

➤ Now after each opportunity you have to take notes with your mind, pause, close your eyes and replay everything you recorded. Say to yourself "My mind's eye will be alert to what appears in my environment at all times. My sub-conscious shall alert me to everything that will protect me from harm and that which enlightens my awareness." Now, open your eyes!

➢ Close your eyes, and concentrate. Once again, say to your-self, "My subconscious mind will alert me to everything that will protect me from harm and that which enlightens my awareness."

Repeat these practices daily until they feel natural and you sense an awareness evolving. I recommend you use the exer-cise as described until you are at ease with it and the outcome you have generated. When you are content with the level of success you have achieved, you may want to consider creating your own exercise to further enhance this skill.

In view of the fact this exercise increases your awareness to the environment where you exist, thus sharpening your psy-chic responsiveness, practicing daily is a key factor in how your ability evolves. In addition, you will be amazed at what you begin to see that had previously gone unnoticed. While it is no longer necessary in today's world for us to have keen surveillance ability, developing the skill will provide you with a protective mechanism that can be used in many different types of circumstances.

As you advance in the practices, visualization will become an integral part of the experience. Taking the time to develop your visualization technique early on will help you achieve a certain level of mastery that will augment future experiences in the advanced practices. The ability to visualize, that is to see without seeing, is one of the most important ingredients to perfecting psychic ability.

Psychic ear has other names; however, for the purpose of this description, I will not fluctuate. I am referring to an ability to hear sound or information that is not in the normal range of human senses. Psychics who have developed their skill are attuned to hear audible messages that others do not experience or see what others cannot. I hear pieces of information, an actual voice, or sound in the environment. In instances, I have answered a telephone but only finding dead silence on the other end. I then receive a message about who was attempting to communicate from the spiritual realm.

One of my female relatives is a fine woman in her eighties. She is certainly a believer in psychic communications, specifically pertaining to communicating with those who have passed over to the spiritual realm. A sister regularly has conversations with this aunt and relays information to me regarding her health and well-being. Shortly after the passing of my aunt's husband, who I will refer to as Fred, he came to me in a dream...laughing. The next morning, when I went downstairs to meditate, my uncle made contact. I heard a laughing and decided to search the house just to make sure it was secure. When I finally went to the kitchen sink to make the morning coffee, a deep cold overwhelmed me. In my mind, I suddenly saw my uncle with one finger over his lips, as if to advise me to be quiet. He appeared to be stealing the peanuts from a dish that was sitting on the stand next to the chair my aunt was occupying. As he moved away, I heard the laughing once again. I knew this was a spiritual communication. I had just had an experience involving the use of my psychic ear. Later, I confirmed my aunt kept a dish of peanuts by her chair. Apparently, my uncle had enjoyed teasing her and took great pleasure in hiding the peanuts.

Several days later, a song and a deep emotion of sorrow overwhelmed me. I personally had no reason to be sad, and I had only heard the song once or twice during my childhood. Startled by what I was experiencing, I asked aloud, "Who is with me?" The spirit, who I will call Ronnie, gave me his name. As soon as I asked the question, the sorrow left me. I was then instructed to call my sister for the answer. When I contacted my sister Helen and explained my experience to her, she informed me that the son of our aunt's close friend had just passed away. After she spoke with my aunt, we learned the son's name was Ronnie and the song was his mother's favorite.

The gift of hearing with a psychic ear is unique. I want to clarify: in my own personal experience, I have never had a conversation with a spirit. The communication in the mind comes through in my own voice and is truly in bits and pieces. However, I will occasionally hear a voice, laughter, or other sounds that come through into the physical world. They appear to be rough gestures by the spiritual world in order to communicate. Given the other side does not have the benefit of vocal cords, what I hear is very different from what I experience in ordinary, everyday communications with the living. Also, you should know the messages or communications I receive from the other side are always positive and are never negative or destructive.

The psychic ear can be developed with patience, concentration, and a high level of awareness. This adeptness is one of many tools that, when mastered, will enhance psychic performance. While some psychics have this experience infrequently, others may use it as a primary method to confer with the other side and provide messages to individuals in the physical world who want to communicate with deceased loved ones. My own abilities are varied. However, all of my senses are engaged during readings. The spiritual realm and universal intelligence will use one method to get one message through; yet, they will use another sense during a different experience. On occasion, all of my senses will be over-whelmed at once by a communication. However, most often, I am using my psychic ear in conjunction with one or more of my senses.

Practice #2: Developing the Hearing

➤ When you are lying in bed, just after practicing your visu-alization, take a moment to listen to all of the sounds around you. Once again, identify the sounds, hear them, and know where they are coming from.

➤ As you settle in, listen carefully. Do you hear the barking of a dog down the street or the wind chimes from the neigh-bor's yard? Perhaps there is music coming from a passing car or the sound of an animal walking across snow or on the deck.

➤ Just as you have started training your mind to be aware of your physical environment visually, you will now train your mind to identify sounds. You will become sensitive to the breathing of a partner lying next to you and the tiptoe-ing of your cat across the carpet. You will hear everything and be able to distinguish it from every other sound.

➤ In your waking hours, do the same practice. Listen, iden-tify, and sensitize your hearing to the environment where you exist. What do you hear? Do you hear the chirping of the crickets before first morning's light or the frogs from a nearby water source? Perhaps you hear the sound of a paper delivery person. What do you hear in the far, distant corners of your world?

➢ Over the course of your day, practice hearing all of the sounds around you, for example, music playing in a passing car, children screaming from a nearby school yard, or the sound of a train whistle from a distant set of tracks.

➢ Develop a full awareness of all of the sounds you are subject to over the course of the day and night, regardless of where you are located.

➢ After you have become sensitive to the sounds in your environment, you will be able to block distracting noise. You will be able to focus on the sounds you choose or those that are of concern to you. While it is advantageous to heighten your awareness of the sounds you experience, the ultimate goal will be to only hear that which is in your best interest.

➢ To make sure you accomplish the goal of sound screening during the course of your practice at night, you will say to yourself, "I am listening to the sounds to familiarize myself with the night. I listen to identify sounds that enhance my psychic ability. I call upon my subconscious to alert me to any sound that I must hear to protect me from harm and/or enhance my psychic ability through communication with intelligence from the other side."

When possible, close your eyes during the initial practices to allow the power of this state to help you achieve mastery. Later on, as you learn more advanced techniques, you will be able to employ your abilities with your eyes open. As you practice, you will discover, because you know what you are doing and how to achieve a certain state, you will be able to shorten and simplify the exercises.

Practice #3: Developing Your Psychic Smell

➤ Start the practice of developing your psychic smell by standing in the middle of a room that is free from distractions each morning and closing your eyes. As you are standing there with your eyes closed, take a deep breath in through your nose. Identify the smells or fragrances you are experiencing as you exhale. Throughout your day, do this in the living room, the kitchen, and the outdoors. As you subsequently encounter new environments, take a moment to pause, smell the air, and familiarize yourself with the different odors associated with the area.

➤ After practicing the ability to stop and familiarize yourself with the odors you experience each day, you will want to become more directed or specific in knowing scents you may encounter. Next, you will go to your own spice rack and smell the individual spices and cooking ingredients you use everyday. Acquaint yourself with the specific bouquet of cinnamon, allspice, mustard, vinegar, coffee, and the various other products you use. Once again, go outside to smell what is blowing through the air, perhaps the scent of blossoms, the smell of freshly mowed grass, or the odor of gasoline from the lawn mower.

➤ Begin to program your subconscious by letting it know, as you identify a scent, you will place this in your memory in order to develop your psychic sense. Remember, be specific when you are planting the familiar scent in your subconscious and identifying the odor.

Many spiritual visitors I experience utilize aromas or scents that are distinctive to them. While I have had numerous encounters in which spirits utilize scent to announce their presence, the story that is most endearing to me involves my mother. Shortly after her death, she started to visit me at night. She filled the bedroom with the scent of her favorite perfume. I sensed she was there to assure me of her presence, and I was pleased she made contact. In an altered state of consciousness, shortly after her visitations began, I felt a deep desire to purchase a lottery ticket. I did so and thus won a small sum of money. However, while I knew my mother was urging me to participate in the drawing, I did not know why she was nudging me to do so. The following morning, my question was answered regarding the lottery. My dog was struck by a truck and sustained life-threatening injuries. I realized the money I had won would pay for her veterinary bills. I knew then my mother was watching over me. In other situations the visitors who have communicated with me used aromas such as, cigarettes, cigars, or pipe tobacco. Some bring the smell of fresh bread with them. Just the other day, in the early morning as I prepared to complete my meditation before a reading, a woman's spirit came to visit and announced her presence with the smell of freshly baked cinnamon rolls. Both my husband and I basked in the aroma knowing someone from the other side was communicating.

Those from the other side often use scents to get my attention and identify themselves for a loved one. As a psychic medium, all of my senses are engaged at varying times during the preparation for readings and during the session. Depending on your development and how you use your skills, you may or may not have this experience regularly in which your sense of smell in engaged. Nevertheless, developing your senses and advancing your ability to engage the psychic smell is important to the overall experience.

Practice #4: Developing the Psychic Feel

➢ Distinguishing between temperature extremes can be accomplished by touching various substances and objects that are hot or cold. Take a small package of frozen meat or frozen food in a solid form from the freezer, and place it in front of you on the counter or table where you are standing. At the same time, pour a cup of coffee (or whatever beverage you drink), and set it next to the frozen food. With one hand, place it on the frozen food. With the other, quickly grasp the cup containing the warm beverage.

➢ Shut your eyes, and feel the significant difference between the two extremes in temperature. (Remember to exercise good judgment. Do not burn your skin.)

➢ Go to your psychic state, and let your subconscious know you are familiarizing yourself with temperature extremes to develop a psychic awareness of the differences.

Again, as a medium, a primary method those from the other side use to get my attention is through an extreme drop in the temperature. The room generally becomes so uncomfortable that no amount of heat or clothing will change the environment. At times, my husband will declare a room is unbearably cold and ask me what is going on. Not only does this happen in the dead of winter when the heat is at full throttle, it also occurs in the middle of summer. The spiritual realm is not shy in announcing its presence by using extreme measures.

Practice developing your awareness of the different sensations you get from temperature differences, smooth surfaces, rough surfaces, as well as liquid and solid substances. Try to remember instances in which you experienced an extreme chill for no reason and considered it an anomaly because there was no other reasonable explanation. Think about what you were involved in at the time and if there were any clues you might have overlooked that would indicate you had a spiritual visitor. After you become more attuned to the temperature differences and other sensations associated with the psychic touch, you might discover something quite different is occurring when a variance in your environment occurs.

Practice #5: The Psychic Touch

➤ Now, you will begin to develop your psychic touch by examining various objects in your environment. The first thing you will need to do is go to the closet where your clothing and shoes are located. Identify the wools, cottons, silks, and leather. Begin touching each and creating what each feels like in your mind. Familiarize yourself with the texture of each item. For instance, is the wool scratchy? Is the leather smooth? Does the cotton have a delicate grain? Do not stop with the closet. Go through your house, and feel the woods, countertops, plants, and glass objects.

➤ When you finish touching the different items in your house and can identify each by touch, stop the exercise. Then relax. Systematically, begin to recall each item and what it felt like. Once you have gone through the list of items you touched, tell your subconscious you are implanting this information to develop your psychic touch.

Practice #6: The Psychic Taste

➢ This is also important in the development of your psychic awareness because it augments your touching, feeling, and smelling faculties. Just as you have familiarized yourself with the other senses you use, taste should be registered with your subconscious as well.

➢ As you ingest your food or liquid, take time to taste the ingredients, sense the temperature, and note the texture. Say to your subconscious that you are registering the food and liquid to enhance your psychic ability. Repeat this practice in conjunction with the other practices until you register what you are experiencing naturally.

CHAPTER 3

The First Stage of Psychic Awareness

Most people can remember an incident in which they knew who was calling before they picked up the telephone or knew an accident was about to occur. They then later dismissed the event as simply an anomaly. For me, my psychic gift has been an integral part of my existence since early childhood. Interacting with the spiritual realm came naturally. At times, I remember thinking the other side was sequentially introducing new experiences to me in order to train me to communicate for them. I came to accept and expect to interact with the spiritual realm. As an adult, I made a decision to study the techniques other psychics used to communicate with the spiritual realm. What became apparent is that my natural experiences corresponded with how others experienced the gift.

In this section, I will explain the process and practices required to achieve a psychic state. As a result, if you successfully complete each, you will accomplish that goal.

Thus far, everything in the practices has played a role in sensitizing your mind to accessing your basic psychic awareness.

You have always been able to do what you learned during the earlier practices. However, with the busy lives we all experience today, you may have dulled these senses or started taking them for granted.

The chakras of the body, the centers of activity, are associated with the colors in a rainbow. Immediately above the crown of our head is a brilliant white light. In the middle of our brow, just above the eyes, is a dove gray color. The throat is represented by purple. Yellow represents the heart. The solar plexus and our sexual organs are represented by lavender. Our feet, which represent the earth, are surrounded by the seven prismatic colors of red, orange, yellow, green, blue, sapphire blue, and lavender/violet. When you engage the use of the color spectrum, as you will learn to do in the practices, it will have a positive effect upon the associated region of the body you empower. You will learn how to call upon and use these colors in utilizing your psychic ability. The next set of practices will require a quiet setting where you will not be disturbed by internal or external distractions.

Practice #1: The Spectrum of Colors

➢ In the space you have set aside to complete your practices, prepare yourself to go into your psychic state. Begin breathing in and out...breathe in and out...breathe in and out. Repeat this until your mind is clear and you are able to focus on your activity.

➢ Close your eyes and then open them.

➢ Next, you will close your eyes. Imagine you are holding several round, fluffy feathers that float so gently ever upward into the sky when you release them and then disappear from sight.

➢ Now imagine you are holding seven feathers that are red, orange, yellow, green, light blue, sapphire, and lavender/violet.

➢ Quietly, release the red feather. Watch it drift into the sky until you can no longer see it. Release the orange feather, the yellow feather, the green feather, the light blue feather, the sapphire feather, and the lavender/violet feather. Watch each until they drift out of sight and into the atmosphere.

➢ After releasing each feather, slowly open your eyes. Repeat the practice until you see each colored feather distinctively and can see it slowly float from sight as a complete, colorful object.

The goal is to train our subconscious to see and allow you to go into a deep state of functioning. Do not be concerned with any difficulty you may have initially in visualizing the feathers or seeing them in full color. The practice may take time to master so that you can visualize the shape and color of the feather completely. So that you can succeed in this practice, at the beginning of each session, make sure you are relaxed and free of interruptions from the outside world. (Remember, start with the plain white feathers and then imagine the feathers in the colors indicated.)

Practice #2: Expanding the Visualization

➢ Return to your practice space, and close your eyes. At the corner of your right eye, you will see the image of a red beach ball drifting across your frontal vision and disappearing on the left side of your mental vision until it completely disappears. Next comes the orange beach ball...the yellow beach ball...the green beach ball...the light blue beach ball...the sapphire beach ball...the lavender/violet beach ball. Each floats from the right side of your vision across the frontal vision and disappearing on the left.

➤ Now, each beach ball begins to return from the left side of your mental vision and in reverse order. First, the lavender/violet beach ball drifts across your vision...the sapphire beach ball...the light blue beach ball...the green beach ball...the yellow beach ball...the orange beach ball...the red beach ball. Each disappears to the left of your mental vision.

➤ It does not stop here. This time, you see perfectly round cotton balls. The first is red, drifting from the right side of your mental vision all the way across your frontal vision and disappearing on the left side of your vision. Then comes the orange cotton ball...the yellow cotton ball...the green cotton ball...the light blue cotton ball...the sapphire cotton ball...the lavender/violet cotton ball. Finally, the lavender/violet cotton ball drifts from the corner of your left mental vision, moving across your frontal vision and disappearing on the right mental vision. Each cotton ball does the same—the sapphire, the light blue, the green, the yellow, the orange, and the red.

In your mind, you have learned to create and visualize the seven colors of the spectrum representing the rainbow or earth center of the body. In addition, you created shapes, formed textures, and controlled the movement. This exercise helps you in relaxation and in taking you to a deeper level in your subconscious.

Practice #3: Going Deeper

➢ Sitting in your practice area where you will not be disturbed by internal or external sources, close your eyes. Taking several minutes to clear your mind of any outside disturbances and relaxing, imagine a bright, illuminating white light setting on the crown of your head. In the center of the bright light, you see the number 7. Allow the bright, glowing light to move down from the top of your head (7) into your brow (6) area just above your eyes. Feel the warmth, and note that it is healing. Your eyes and face relax as it moves into your throat (5). Feel the warmth surrounding you in the neck as it moves into your heart (4) and then your abdomen (3). As it circulates the warmth and calms your internal organs, it moves into the area of your pelvis and sexual organs (2). Continue to relax as the heat moves in your legs and ends at your feet (1).

➢ The brilliant white light with the bright yellow center moves up and around the outside of your body until it re-forms into a ball on the crown of your head. Again, it moves through your body. It moves from the crown into the brow area just above the eyes then into your throat and then your heart, abdomen, pelvis and sex organs. It ends at your feet, where it exits. It then comes back up around the outside of your body, forming in a ball of brilliant white light on the top of your head.

➢ This is the third energy ball that flows through your body. It starts at the crown of your head moving into the brow area just above the eyes and then into your throat, heart, abdomen, pelvis and sex organs. It ends in at your feet. It then circles up to the top of your head, leaving you in a state of total relaxation.

➤ Speak to your subconscious now. Tell yourself that, from this day forward, in order to reach this state of psychic relaxation, you only need to count backwards from seven to one. Now you are completely relaxed.

➤ Now, it is time to open your eyes. Know you can reach this state of psychic relaxation at any time by simply counting backwards from seven to one.

This practice will help you to move your mental state to a basic psychic level. You have learned how to program the mind through the utilization of your visualization abilities by expanding the practice in Chapter 2. Now it is time to learn how to program your subconscious to achieve a deeper psychic state using more complex methods. To prepare for the next practices, refresh yourself on what you have learned so far. Then read through each of the next practices several times so that you completely understand what you need to do during the session.

Practice #4: The Psychic State

➤ By now, you recognize why it is necessary to develop a special place to practice where you will not be disturbed by internal or external sources. Go to your practice space, establish yourself in a comfortable position, and engage in a relaxation practice. After you are completely relaxed, before beginning, read this practice as many times as you feel necessary.

➤ Close your eyes, and begin.

➤ You are on a path leading down a gentle hill. Notice there are steps on the path. As you take a step down, say to yourself, "I am moving down into a deeper psychic state."

Continue to walk down each step, noticing there are ten. With each step, say, "I am moving down into a deeper psychic state." Step down until you reach the bottom step (which is one) and say, "I can come to this psychic state whenever I choose by counting down—ten, nine, eight, seven, six, five, four, three, two, and one."

➤ Now open your eyes. Repeat the practice with your eyes open.

➤ Remember your development and continued success is based on practicing. This practice should be completed at least once per week in conjunction with your other practices during your first three months of learning.

The key to your future development will be in practicing faithfully what you learn. Each day, look for opportunities to utilize your skills in some way. Always begin by going to your basic psychic level before you engage in an activity. One of the first psychic pursuits you can engage in will involve bringing someone you are thinking about into your mental vision. Imagine them standing or setting with you and then ask the person to talk with you for a while. Tell the person you want to know something that is important to them. In some cases, you might receive an important message about the person or information on something they are about to experience that they do not know about. In other instances, a spirit wanting to make contact with that person or their guardian angel may join you.

As a psychic, I open a channel for those on the other side to communicate with me daily. However, just before a reading, I take special care to prepare for the session by going to my deepest psychic level to invite those from the other side to join me and identify themselves. As spirits present themselves to me, they bring forth their image, information about who will be attending the session, and messages they want delivered to a loved one. In many instances, this information is quite specific. For example, I am presented with images showing the hair color of a person who will be attending the session, the type of clothing he or she will be wearing, or the color of his or her eyes. In conjunction with the images, I will hear certain things about a person relating to a personal matter that only they will recognize or hear his or her name.

As I have explained repeatedly, developing each of your senses is important. When I prepare for a psychic session, I awaken all of my senses so that I am available to receive any type of message that comes through from the spiritual realm. I will smell a fragrance in conjunction with a visual image, see a snapshot, or hear a name. Except for temperature variations, which occur consistently and are associated with a spiritual presence, each time I invite the spiritual realm to communicate its methods for delivering a message are different. There is no communication standard established for the other side, so it is important to expect the unexpected.

Each person who pursues the development of his or her psychic ability will evolve differently. However, once again, it is important to develop each of your senses so that you are prepared to receive a message when the opportunity arises and understand what is occurring.

Chapter 4

White Aura of Protection

Once you begin your the journey through the world using psychic wandering, communications, and astral projection, you can expect to have both positive and negative experiences. Preparing for each is essential to your personal well-being. It is critical you understand your power and you will bring into your psychic consciousnesses whatever you choose. You alone decide what will show up in your subconscious. No one else can implant something you have not made possible. An individual programs his or her mind and creates the reality of choice. When you plant information or suggestions in your subconscious that leads to a desired goal, your mind will begin to move you toward implementation. You will achieve the goals you set out to accomplish in some form.

I do not want to suggest the information and experiences we have daily with the external world cannot infiltrate our thinking and, in some way, interfere with the goals we establish or the view we have of ourselves. However, this influence can only affect our subconscious programming if we allow the intruders to get in and disrupt our plan. Messages or information that should command our attention will come from our guardian angels or what I refer to as "Spiritual Mentors." These messages can be a warning we need to heed regarding something that will harm us or about something positive that will assist us in some way. For example, my garage door opener is new and has been thoroughly inspected. One afternoon, when my husband and I were scheduled to attend a friend's retirement party, I decided to run an errand before the affair. For some reason, I grabbed a set of spare car keys that did not have the house keys attached. When I returned to the house after completing the errand, the garage door would not open. I had no way of entering the house. I still had to get ready for the evening, and my husband had left his office for the day. The only thing I could do was wait for him to arrive and hope we would not be too late for the party. When he arrived, as if by magic, the garage door opened. Nothing appeared to be wrong with the device. Unclear about why my garage door opener failed, I started to sense we were supposed to arrive respectfully late to the affair. We finally departed, knowing we would be at least forty-five minutes late. As we turned onto the road leading to the drive-way for the friend's home, we encountered a multiple-car accident that had resulted in several injuries and a death. If we had left at the original time, we quite possibly would have been involved in the accident that had occurred forty minutes before we arrived on the scene. After this incident, the garage door was fine. I felt as though my guardian had intervened to keep my husband and me from being injured or killed.

Keeping in mind that you will want to receive messages that will keep you from harm, warning you of potential dangers in addition to the positive information that comes to you while blocking negative thoughts that are destructive, I am going to teach you some methodology to program your subconscious to do just that. Remember, positive energy will attract positive energy. Negative energy will attract negative energy. Because what we encounter in the external world can be less than kind or positive, it is important to learn how to cast aside negative thinking that can poison your mind and allow negative energy from the other side to seep in. When negative energy clouds our perception it can easily influence how we treat others and ourselves.

In the next practice, you will learn to program your sub-conscious to immediately deny negative energy access and cause it to dissipate without harming others. The creation of an energy force formed from a brilliant white light will sur-round you at all times. It will serve as a shield that reflects negative energy away from you, thereby causing it to simply dissolve into the universe.

I believe that each of us experiences multiple lives. Each time we are born, we come with a mission to accomplish. It is important we do not negatively affect others during the course of our experience. While there are times we inadver-tently cause others pain out of ignorance, it is important that it not be purposeful. The universe is forgiving in the case of ignorance, but it is not when we knowingly commit a nega-tive act against someone. If you act in a harmful way against others, you may find that what goes around will come around. If not in this lifetime, it will occur in the next. Consequently, in this opportunity you have created by devel-oping your psychic awareness, it is important to protect your-self and others from negative influences. Creating the shield will protect you from negative energy that could lead you to take actions that harm others. It will also allow you to shield others from negative influences.

Practice #1: The Power of White Light, Shielding

➤ In your special place of practice, you will want to perform what I refer to as the rite of "Surroundings Separation and Distinction." The place you use to do your practices can be used for other purposes. However, it is important to do a blessing of the area or rite of "Separation and Distinction" to bring about the peace and security you need to complete the work. If you do use the space for other purposes, the rite will calm the area for those purposes as well.

➤ Stand in the space, and go to your deep psychic level by imagining a brilliant, illuminating white light surrounding your body. When you symbolically touch an area in the space you use, you can feel the positive energy you release. Imagine the energy begins to encircle the entire room, forming a protective ring from all negative energy and harm.

➤ Now, as you feel the warm, energy surrounding the room and your body, say aloud, "In this space, the power of the white light shall protect me. Only the energy of the white light may enter this room. All that is negative will dissipate simply by touching the energy."

➤ Extend your hand—arm straight out from your body—and trace the boundaries of the room, once again creating a circle with the energy of the white light. Allow yourself to feel the protective power of the light as you release it into the space. Make sure to complete the ring of protection by bringing it completely together.

➤ Look up at the ceiling, and extend your hand and arm. Begin releasing your energy, and ask the light to fill in the room outside of the circle.

➤ Relax. Know this space is protected. You need not perform this rite again unless others access your space.

Practice #2: Creating a Personal Shield

➤ In your practice space, which is free from internal and external interruptions, make yourself comfortable. Close your eyes.

➤ Closing your eyes, go to the basic psychic level. See yourself standing in front of you.

➤ Remembering the power of the brilliant white light, allow it once again to surround your body. Feel the warmth and comfort the light provides as it encircles your entire body.

➤ Speak to your subconscious. Let it know this is a powerful and positive energy force that acts as your shield, repelling all negative energy and thoughts from your mind.

➤ Say to yourself, "This protective light surrounds me and will remain with me permanently." Tell your subconscious to be vigilant in identifying negative thoughts and energy that attempt to infiltrate your mind and/or negative thoughts that others may attempt to implant.

➤ Say to yourself, "I can deny negative thoughts access to my mind by saying, 'No, I do not think this or this way. Be gone!'" The power of the white light will immediately cancel the negative thought and cause it to dissipate, thus allowing your thinking to return to positive.

➤ Now open your eyes. Feel the warmth and comfort of the white light. Know you are safe.

The day after completing the practices to shield your body and practice space, return to the space. Close your eyes, and bring yourself forward. As you come into your mental view, the first thing you should see is the brilliant white shield of protection surrounding your body. If you do not see the shield, repeat the practice as often as necessary until your shield is always in place. When the shield appears automatically, you no longer need to do the practice. Next, remember what comes with the shield, the power to cause any negative thinking or energy to dissipate by just saying no. Now, each time you enact the white light power of saying no to repel negative energy and your result is positive, pause. Congratulate your subconscious. Let it know the method was successful.

The shield surrounding your body will always be in place once it is successfully implanted in your subconscious. You will need to remember to invoke its power when you feel negative thoughts are coming through. Even in the most innocent circumstances involving negativity, shield yourself. Observe how your interaction with others changes. However, you will periodically want to evoke the white light in your place of practice. In particular, if others access the space regularly, you will want to complete the process at least once per month.

CHAPTER 5

Becoming a Psychic: Responsibilities and Tribulations

As a psychic medium, my ability to channel information from the spiritual realm and intelligent universe has allowed me to know an outcome before an event happened, a probable diagnosis in issues relating to health, or what was occurring in someone's relationship. Because of the type of information I receive, I have always approached my gift with respect. Early on in my life, depending on the information that came through to me regarding their situation, I realized I could have a positive or negative impact on the lives of others. Having access to this type of information has forced me to develop a sense of responsibility regarding how to use the information and under what circumstances. I learned, just because the other side, my spirit mentors, guardian angels, and those who had passed over provided me with information, it did not mean I had to share what I knew. This is an important part of becoming a psychic because each of us must consider how information will ultimately affect someone's life. When you provide an insight, it should have a positive impact on the lives it will touch. If it does not, think about minding your own business. While you might think providing someone with a piece of information regarding a spouse or health will set them free, it could have exactly the opposite effect. Therefore, before you share information, you will need to be certain you are doing so because those on the other side are directing you to share. Always pause to ask your spirit mentor or guardian angel if you should provide someone with information that will have a dramatic impact on his or her lives. Use the following rule of thumb: If you hesitate or feel uncomfortable, ask the other side for advice on what to do with the information you receive. Remember to listen with your psychic hearing for answers from the other side. Do not allow your ego or the need to share information influence your decisions.

Thus far, with the practices, you have learned how to attain a psychic level that will allow you to explore many different psychic experiences. If you choose to complete the practices faithfully and hone your skills, the universe is yours to discover. If you decide to use your ability professionally, this will be a rewarding undertaking. It is one that requires an intense level of dedication. It will be important to examine your motives and know yourself completely before engaging in the activity with others. Once again, there are many choices you will need to make regarding information, such as when it should be shared and with whom. A psychic should take his or her gift seriously, respecting those on the other side who assist us in the physical world and those residing in this world who can be vulnerable.

Each practice I have shared so far is standard and designed to awaken your psychic abilities. How each of us responds to the learning will be different. Remember, each of us is here in the physical world for a purpose. I sincerely believe we are on a mission to complete part of the journey towards infinite knowledge. I have used my own skills naturally from an early age and never received formal training. As an adult, I became curious about what other psychics had done to develop their gift. When I started to read information specifically related to the development of psychic ability, I quickly learned my natural ability closely resembled the teachings. Many of you will find that what you learn through the practices is not new and you are naturally achieving a psychic state. Others will develop to a certain point and then move on to other things. Some will not be able to achieve the level of psychic awareness they had hoped. I believe success in developing psychic skills is related to our previous lives and our current mission. If developing your psychic ability is part of your life plan, you will not be able to avoid this from happening. However, if it distracts you from accomplishing what you are here to achieve, you may not be successful.

When you have decided to enter the world of psychics and to practice, many different situations involving the activities associated with this gift can take place. Preparing yourself for the possibilities will allow you to deal with unusual experiences and not be frightened or concerned. I was raised in a home in which my parents and several siblings had psychic ability. Spirit visitors were regulars in my home. As a result, I was never really startled by the various methods they used to communicate, including materialization.

In the spring of 2004, I was completing a chapter in a book I was writing when I became overwhelmed by an urgency related to a dear friend of my oldest sister. I will call him John. For several months, I had sensed he was experiencing health problems that would threaten his life. I had suggested my sister prepare herself for bad news related to his condition. I needed to clarify, if possible, what I was sensing. I went into a deep psychic state to ask my spirit mentor to tell me about John's medical condition. On one other occasion, during a deep psychic state, my spirit guide had used my uncle who had died from leukemia to infer that someone suffered from a similar condition. This time, I was shown a scene in which my uncle was sitting in a chair next to John. Several weeks passed, my oldest sister called to let me know that John had been diagnosed with a rare blood disease. I asked her if it was leukemia, and she assured me it was a blood disease. After several months had passed, my sister called me and said she had just learned that John had been misdiagnosed the first time. In fact, he did have a form of leukemia.

There is a message in the next story that will prepare you for various situations you encounter. You will perhaps have this type of encounter and others that may be far harder to deal with than you can imagine. Several years ago, one of my younger sisters passed away from an aggressive cancer. Before anyone knew she did not have long to live, I had a dream that provided me with the date of her death and directed me to support her in the treatment decisions she would make. I did not tell her what I saw and supported her decisions regarding treatment. I chose to send as much healing and loving energy to her as was possible. What I noticed is that, as I would send healing toward her, I would be brought back to the message that I needed to support her in her transition to the other side. The experience was quite painful, and I wanted desperately to let her know that her situation was dire. When I look back at how she handled her life during those final months, she did so with dignity and a feeling of self-power. She was a strong, proud woman who had always been in control. If I had given her the message that she did not have long to live, she would perhaps have died much sooner. I recognized I did not have the right to take anything away from her and the best thing to do was support her in every decision she made.

When you are a practicing psychic, you will be a conduit for an array of encounters and messages. You can learn to cope with most situations and will come to naturally discern when sharing information is appropriate. Unfortunately, using the information you possess will not always be possible or of benefit to the individual of interest. Just remember, there is a power in the universe much greater than we are. You will also not be able to alter plans that must be implemented. I was moved away from committing energy to healing my sister psychically. In fact, I was shown the month and year of her death. In two dreams, my mother, father, and brother came to me regarding the impending death of my sister. One situation was to encourage me to let go; another was to let me know her death was imminent. The universal intelligence knew about the mission she came to accomplish and her death was part of that plan.

Just as I have given you the practice, which trains you on how to surround your practice space and body with white light protection, you can go to your deepest psychic level and surround anyone. Sending positive energy into the world is generally a good thing to do. When you do this as part of your practices, it increases your own power to send forth the healing and protection of the white light when you feel it is most urgent.

Again, as a medium communicating with the other side, it often involves the use of symbols, words, and other clues requiring some form of interpretation. In the case of my sister, my brother took me to a hospital-like setting that was very cold. Everyone was pale. As I drifted with him, I saw my sister in a room with his widow. Both looked through me as if I did not exist. Later, after the death of my sister, my brother's widow was diagnosed with the same cancer my sister had. My brother had provided me with a vision of my sister's death as well as provided me with information regarding his widow. In the case of John, my oldest sister's friend, when I had the vision of my deceased uncle who died of leukemia sitting next to him in a chair, this was an indicator the two had the same disease.

While you can receive many different types of communication that require you to look at the information you receive and complete the puzzle, do not assume anything or interrupt information literally. Seeing a death card, for example, may not mean a person will die. It can mean that something is about to change in the person's life. On the other hand, it can denote the death of a relationship or addiction. This is why we must use caution in this profession. The world interrupted through psychic perspective is anything but usual, and nothings as it seems. Identifying each piece of information that comes through, establishing who the message is for and then attempting to figure out an exact meaning is not easy. Learn to respect each communication from the other side and become vigilant in protecting those who seek information. The consequences on the human psychic can be devastating if we provide someone with a misinterpreted message or a message they are not ready to receive.

Now that you have had psychic experiences and have some concept of what occurs in the world of psychics, it is important to remember certain things. Most importantly, thought-like vibration is an emanating energy that does not cease to exist simply by wishing it to be so. Once a thought occurs, it goes forward to create that which it describes. Learning to form your thoughts and keep them positive will not only assist you in attaining the results you desire. It will also help you attain a more complete conversation with the other side.

To go to your psychic level of awareness, you must alter your state of mind and slow your thinking so that you can become focused. When you close your eyes, you can achieve this state quicker than when your eyes are open. You can thus use your skill faster. Through the practice of forming complete visual images in your mind, you can create yet another means to access psychic ability and boost your awareness in the psychic state. Once more, understanding our mission in this life is important because it will provide us with perspective on how the gift fits into that plan. Each person is born with a psychic ability and can be trained to achieve a basic psychic level of functioning. How you choose to utilize the gift or to what extent you develop the skill will depend on what you are intended to pursue in this life.

The universe is a connected system of energy. For every action, there is a reaction. Moreover, our thoughts play a role in this construct. What we think moves forward in the world and affects someone or something else in the world. Sending positive thoughts is not a guarantee you will always receive positive thoughts in return. However, producing negative thought almost certainly promises, at some point, you will have negative energy directed at you. Remember to say no to negative thought and surround yourself with the brilliant white light.

Becoming a psychic is possible with the practices you have learned thus far. The entire process, however, is much more complex and entails more than closing your eyes. You must train your mind through repetition. To spontaneously reach each part of our psychic awareness, the mind must know what is expected. When your mind is sufficiently trained through repetition, it comes to know how to function. Again, in some cases, the ability will come easily. For others, it will take time.

The subconscious mind is a special place with unique abilities based on the type of brain activity that occurs. When you close your eyes, the brain automatically slows down and generates activity that allows us to access our subconscious mind. The subconscious mind is available for training and does exactly what it is told to do. This is the place where you create dreams, imagine how to get there, and command the subconscious to make it happen. The subconscious then obeys us. In turn, it begins to implement our plan. If you tell yourself that you can train successfully for a marathon and run the marathon to completion, you will begin to develop a plan of action to get there. The subconscious then will implement the plan. On the other hand, if you tell yourself you are far too frail and lack the athletic ability to ever run a marathon, your subconscious mind will believe this to be true as well.

I do believe your psychic development is in your hands if it is part of your overall mission in life. The key to your success will be in your desire and commitment to the practices. Repetition is necessary in learning what is necessary to move forward with your gift.

Becoming a professional in this field requires commitment and compassion. Part of what you will do is listening to your client. Most of what you will eventually do is listening to the messages from your spiritual mentors, guardian angels, and those who have passed over to the other side. The messages you will receive may involve the need to interrupt information that is less than clear. Remember, your clients have a role to play in the reading as much as you and all of the players on the other side do. Learn how to engage your client in the process, and make sure everyone understands that even the best psychic is not always right.

CHAPTER 6

Prophecy and Clairvoyance

The ability to perceive all that exists outside of the natural range of human senses is referred to as clairvoyance. This involves experiencing keen intuitive insights or an ability to act in a discriminating way regarding perceptions that you receive. Therefore, one can foresee the future and predict what will occur in a certain situation or for an individual in certain set of circumstances. Psychics regularly utilize clairvoyance in their work. As you have experienced in the practices, learning to go to your basic psychic level allows you to hear messages from your spiritual mentor, guardian angel, or those who have passed over.

Many people have experienced a nagging feeling that something was about to happen and, in some instances, what will occur and to whom. This perhaps is one of our ancient means of interacting before the advent of verbal and written communication. As other acts of sharing information evolved, it became increasingly less necessary to communicate through natural methods.

In this age of constant communication and hurried lifestyles, clairvoyance is not considered useful. This method of interaction with others is not thought to be an efficient use of one's time, if you choose to use the gift. However, the issue is not just about developing a preference for how we communicate or use our time. There are obstacles that an individual will face if they chose to develop their gift. The most obvious is the existing persona that suggests only those individuals born with the gift have the ability to successfully engage in the art. Perhaps the biggest obstacle of all however, has been created by religion and the entertainment industry. Each has vilified individuals who engage in psychic activities portraying the art as dark and, in many cases, evil. As a consequence, many people reject the possibility that they could utilize the ability fearing criticism or the possibility of being stigmatized. The truth in this matter is that everyone has a certain level of clairvoyance. The gift is natural, certainly not mystical or evil.

Again, the choice to develop and use clairvoyance has more to do with our current mission on earth. If you are intended to develop the gift and use it successfully, you will create the opportunity. Alternatively, the opportunity will present itself if your plan demands that you utilize your psychic ability.

The next set of practices will allow you to awaken your clairvoyance and develop a better understanding of yourself. The ability to visualize and commit certain information to memory is an important technique to use. While this is one more tool and level you will encounter on the way to becoming a psychic, it is just one more building block you need to add. Each of the following practices will positively program your subconscious to create something from nothing anytime you choose. Remember to complete one practice per session.

Repeat each practice one time per week until you are comfortable with the outcome.

Practice #1: Creating an Image from Nothing

➢ In your protected practice space, free from internal and external interruptions, close your eyes. Relax, and clear your mind of any thoughts about your day so that you can focus on the practice. When you are relaxed, go to your basic psychic level.

➢ Imagine you are in room with a stark white wall in front of you. A black felt pin and an eraser are sitting in a tray on the table beside the wall.

➢ Walk over to the tray. Pick up the black felt pen and draw a large square.

➢ Inside the square, print your name.

➢ Step back. Look at the square and your name.

➢ Now step back up to the board. Sit the pen back in the tray, and pick up the eraser.

➢ Erase your name without touching the lines of the square. Say to yourself, "I can visualize anything I want to see at any time I choose." Erase the square, and open your eyes.

Practice #2: Painter in the Clouds

➢ Go to your protected practice place, free from internal and external interruptions, and close your eyes. Relax, and clear your mind of any thought about your day so that you can focus on the practice. When you are relaxed, go to your basic psychic level.

➢ See yourself standing on scaffolding next to the sky. The platform sways ever so gently, and you feel completely secure standing there as it moves from side to side slowly across the sky.

➢ A giant bucket of white paint is beside you. A large paint-brush that is light as a feather is in your hand.

➢ Take the brush, dip it into the paint, and slowly write your name across the sky as the platform moves to your right.

➢ When you have finished, as the platform moves to your left, it stops. You can see your name painted on the light blue sky.

➢ Gently, a light wind comes up and blows the soft white, marshmallow paint away. It disappears into the clouds.

➢ Speak to your subconscious, saying, "I am becoming a better psychic each time I perform this visualization." Open your eyes.

Practice #3: Seeing Your Body through the Mental Eye

➢ Go to your protected practice place, free from internal and external distractions. Relax, and clear your mind of any thought about your day so that you can focus on the practice. Now close your eyes, and go to your basic psychic level.

➢ Bring forth your image, and look at every part of your body. See your hair, nose, and the shape of your chin. See your body, and note how everything looks, including your long arms and legs. See yourself in detail.

➢ Look closely at yourself, saying, "I can bring the presence of any creature, entity or person into my psychic mental vision merely by asking the creature, entity or person to appear to me."

➤ Open your eyes.

At times, the work you will complete as a psychic will involve asking the individual you want to communicate with to come forward. Before a session, I go to a deep psychic state. I invite spirits who want to speak with me to come forward. When I am finished, I thank the spirits for communicating with me and ask my spirit mentor and guardian angel to come forward. I ask my spirit mentor and guardian angel to provide me with insight about the spirits who came through to speak to their loved ones. In each situation, I receive a wealth of information about those who have passed over and those in the physical world who will be attending the session. As you become more comfortable with communicating psychically you will find that you are able to communicate with the living as well as those who have passed over to the other side.

Imagining your body in complete detail will help you to become open-minded in looking at the physical body. This will also train your subconscious to look at the detail associated with any image or information that comes to mind. As part of your initial practices I suggested that you attempt to communicate with someone you were thinking about and ask them questions. Establishing this psychic link in an attempt to communicate is not intrusive. Attempting to make the connection is part of your practices. The psychic's link with the human being, creature, angel, spiritual mentor, spirit from the other side, or entity opens your line of communication. While the image that comes forward to you will not always look exactly like who or what you are communicating with, it will provide you with a basic idea of their image. In some cases, I will only see hair and eyes or the shape of a body.

However, when I use this visualization practice, I will also receive other clues that let me know who I am communicating with.

Clairvoyance requires focus. Because this is the most important factor in developing your innate psychic ability, you will need to take the practices designed to assist you in developing this skill seriously. Practice each faithfully. Another important component to developing this part of your gift is to pay close attention to the hunches you have and the feelings or intuition about certain things. Listening carefully will further reinforce that you want to be a psychic to your mind or subconscious.

When you have honed your clairvoyance through the practices, all you will need to do is go to your basic psychic level by relaxing. Focus your awareness on the information you need to know, and it will be provided to you. The universal messages and knowledge will be readily and immediately made available to you. The hunches and intuition about certain things will flow like wine from an open tap. Once again, this profession does have a downside, and that is knowing too much information. At one point in my career as a manager in a large social service agency, my superior asked me to stop telling her what would happen before it occurred. She was unnerved by my capability. You will also experience knowing that something is about to happen and will attempt to share the information. However, you will soon learn that individuals who do not solicit your services are not necessarily enamored with your skills. In many circumstances people do not want to hear the information you are able to share. Remember, each person will learn exactly what he or she needs to know at the right moment and use it in accordance with his or her life plan. This means, if you encounter situations in which individuals simply do not want to hear your message, understand the universe is not ready for them to know what you know. As a psychic, you can occasionally intervene and prevent something disastrous from occurring. However, if something is supposed to happen, it will occur.

Once again, adding building blocks to your knowledge base is important to the development of one's clairvoyant ability. You have learned practices designed to train your mind and program it to develop your psychic awareness. Now it is time to add new practices designed to test your ability and to push you toward making a deeper commitment to skill development in order to focus the training. Remember to complete one practice per session. Repeat each practice one time per week until you are comfortable with the outcome.

Practice #4: Divining

➤ Go to your protected practice place, free from internal and external distractions, and bring a dictionary.

➤ Place the dictionary in front of you on a table, your lap, or the floor where you are sitting.

➤ Relax, and clear your mind of any thought about your day so that you can focus on the practice. Now close your eyes, and go to your basic psychic level of awareness. Ask any question you choose aloud.

➤ With your eyes closed, turn the pages back and forth, allowing the process to occur freely. This can take several minutes.

➤ When you feel you have reached the right spot in the dictionary, plant your finger on the section. Open your eyes, and look at the word.

➢ Keeping your finger on the spot and read the definitions. In the body of the definition, you will find a clue or answer to your question.

➢ Keep a diary of your questions and the answers. As I often say during a reading, the information that comes through may not mean anything at the time you receive it. However, it might the next day.

For example, each of us is curious about our career, family, or other activities in life. You might ask the question, "Will I be a successful psychic?" As you turn through the pages in the dictionary, you come to the word "undeniably." Your finger stops. Most certainly, it would seem, based on the definition of the word, you will become a successful psychic. However, this only refers to your competency. Remember to ask the question (if it is important to you): Will I benefit financially from the profession.

You will next try a method of divination that has been used throughout the ages by the wise, those who were the medicine givers and spiritualists. I have known some people who use it only to predict the sex of a child while others purport to use it in the telling of fortunes. The intent is for you to develop concentration and sense what the other side communicates. Psychic communication again incorporates the usage of all senses and not just one. So let's begin.

Practice #5: An Ornament Suspended

➢ In your practice space, bring a piece of stiff paper or cardboard, a black felt pen, and a piece of twine or yarn with a heavy object secured to one end (for example, a medallion, heavy gem, or other object that significantly distinguishes the bottom of the string from the top). As you sit in a comfortable position, place the paper or cardboard in front of you. Draw a line one way and then the other, leaving an inch of margin on the top and side. Write "Yes" at the top and bottom of the page (the vertical line). Write "No" at the side (the horizontal line).

➢
Yes

No + No

Yes

➢ Take a moment to suspend the ornament over the middle of the diagram without touching the paper. The ornament should be directly over the crisscrossed lines.

➢ Close your eyes, and go to your basic psychic level. Allow yourself a few minutes to relax and feel the weight of the ornament on the string.

➢ Open your eyes, and cause the string to swing back and forth as well as up and down.

➢ As you sense the ornament swinging, state aloud, "When the ornament moves straight up and down, this means yes." Then allow the ornament to swing up and down in a straight line. Then say, "When the ornament swings back and forth from side to side, this means no. Then allow the ornament to sway from side to side."

➢ Stop the ornament from swinging, and remain relaxed. Hold the light end of the string in one hand. Once again, suspend it at the crisscross of the diagram.

➢ State a "yes" or "no" question aloud. You will begin to sense the sway of the ornament in one direction or the other as long as you have asked a "yes" or "no" question. If it swings up and down, the answer is yes. If it swings from side to side, the answer is no.

➤ There will be times when the question cannot be answered and the ornament will swing in a circle. Be sure you have asked a "yes" or "no" question. If you have asked a specific question and the ornament continues to swing in a circle, once again, it means there is no answer at this time.

Remember, questions such as "Will my boss like me tomorrow if I wear yellow and then blue the next day?" requires a more complex answer, if it can be answered at all.

Again, keep a journal specifically dedicated to each practice in which you ask questions. Write down the question and the response as well as the date. Review the responses monthly, and think about what you have experienced that relates to the question and the response.

In the next practices, you will find that each is common in testing the skills of beginning psychics. Many of the Internet sites inviting you to test your psychic skill do so using cards or pictures. In these situations, you are required to identify what is on a set of pictures or images on cards by using your psychic ability. For our purposes in the following practices, you will be using a common set of playing cards. The first practice will involve determining the color of the card without the benefit of seeing the card. The second will involve identifying the card suits.

Practice #6: Card Colors

➤ In your practice place that is safe from internal and external distractions, bring a deck of cards complete with twenty-six red and twenty-six black cards. Also, bring a plain piece of white paper and a felt pen. Place both in front of you. Shuffle the deck, and sit it in front of you. The suits should be facing down at the bottom of the paper. Taking the felt pen, draw a line down the center of the paper. Mark one side as red and the other side as black. Looking at the deck, imagine yourself seeing the cards.

➢ Now close your eyes. Relax, and clear your mind of any thought about your day so that you can focus on the practice. When you feel completely relaxed, go to your basic psychic level. Relax here for a moment. Then open your eyes.

➢ Think about the first card. Then picking it up with the suit away from you so that you cannot see the features of card, ask aloud, "What color am I holding?" Listen for the first answer. If correct, place a mark on the paper under the color that is correct. Remember, establish a pile for those you identify correctly and those you identify incorrectly.

➢ If possible, go through this practice twice during each setting. However, do not become fatigued. During the first setting, I will usually get thirty-eight cards correct. During the second practice in the setting, as my mind begins to tire, I will get only thirty-two cards correct. The key is to build your stamina and gradually increase the number of times you complete the practice during each setting before tiring the mind. Initially, as you begin to learn the technique, if you feel one practice is all you can do efficiently, then listen to your inner voice.

Practice #7: Card Suits

> ➤ Once again, go to your practice place that is free of internal and external distractions. Bring a complete deck of fifty-two cards, a plain piece of paper, and a felt pen. There are four suits or symbols in a card deck: heart, spade, diamond, and club. Shuffle the deck. Place it facedown in front of you. Taking the paper, lay it just above the card and divide it into four equal squares.

> ➤ Relax. Clear your mind of any thought about your day so that you can focus on the practice. When you feel completely relaxed, go to your basic psychic level. Stay a few minutes, and relax. Opening your eyes, look at the deck in front of you. Picking up the first card with the face pointed away from you, ask, "What is the suit of this card?" Before responding, wait and listen. Think about what you are holding.

> ➤ Turn the card toward you. If you were correct, place one mark on the paper under the proper suit. Remember to keep two separate piles: one for your correct answers and one for the incorrect.

You will go through the entire deck and count the number correct when you finish. If you obtained a score of thirteen or more, your psychic sensing and psychic communication is active. Once again, complete the practice at least twice. Then allow your mind to rest. Building up to repeated practices within a setting is important. Just as you would do in preparation to master any subject or interest in life you might pursue, it will take a while before you perfect the technique associated with this mental challenge. Be patient and persistent in embarking upon the practices and in completing each.

CHAPTER 7

Sending and Receiving Information Using Mental Telepathy

The phenomenon known as telepathy involves a communication between minds. The sending and receiving of information between two people can include thoughts, words, images, and a sensation or dreams. Often described as "thought transfer," the act of telepathic communication has been written about in the lore of many societies for thousands of years. Unfortunately, the gift took on new meaning in the twentieth century and was often portrayed as a manipulative act used by elderly women known as fortune-tellers and spiritualists who communicated with the dead. The gift was given a bit more credibility as psychologists began to study the phenomenon. It was then accepted as something that did occur among certain people. However, the art was still met with criticism. Most people continued to be of the opinion that only emotional woman and mentally fragile elderly participated in such activities. In some situations, groups have developed other names for the ability. The founders declare their methods, which involve the use of an individual's psychic ability, are something quite different. I assume their intent was to create an illusion they were doing something new and to distance themselves from an established profession. The truth is, regardless of what you choose to call the skill, with practice, both sexes and people of all ages are capable of developing their psychic gift.

The use of telepathic senses or powers can be extraordinary and, in some cases, supernatural in nature. As a medium, I receive messages from those who are deceased; however, I also receive messages from the living. I have always had the ability to know who was calling just before the telephone would ring. Finishing a sentence for someone has little to do with familiarity. It has more to do with the receipt of information transmitted by that individual. This psychic method is similar to clairvoyance or clairaudience. As I described for you previously, clairvoyance involves the ability to see objects, have visions, or gain knowledge regardless of the distance involved. Clairaudience involves the ability to hear things everywhere.

My husband and I are extremely close and definitely communicate naturally through telepathy. Whether it is about him not feeling well, having a difficult workday, or desiring a specific meal, I seem to know what he is thinking. In turn, he knows my thoughts as well. What we have is not unusual, even though our experience with this type of interaction probably occurs more frequently than with many couples who share the ability. I believe, in our case, we are emotionally synchronized to have this level of psychic communication. Consequently, it comes naturally. However, once again, many people do not accept or practice the use of this skill. Thus, this type of communication between individuals who are emotionally in harmony is probably dismissed as coincidental.

Deciding to use the method with intention is, of course, quite possible. As with any other technique you have learned so far during the practices, this can also be programmed into your subconscious. You should consider it as yet another tool you will store and use to increase your psychic ability.

By now, you have learned that repetition and focus in completing the practices have allowed you to access your deepest psyche. To develop your telepathic ability, you will need a set of cards containing pictures of people, objects, scenery, and animals. You may want to create your own cards by cutting images from magazines and pasting each onto a heavy white piece of paper, (be sure to construct the cards so that they are easy to handle.) Whether you choose to purchase the cards or create them, this practice will require two sets of cards. Each set will include thirty-two cards and will include eight different pictures of the four categories: people, objects, scenery, and animals. In addition, as part of this practice, you will require a partner. One person sends a message as he or she visualizes the picture on the card they hold while the other person receives the message.

Practice #1: Sending and Receiving

➤ You and your partner enter your practice place that is safe from internal and external distractions. Sitting across from one another, the sender will shuffle the cards and place them facedown on the surface between the sender and receiver. The receiver will bring several sheets of plain paper and a pen. These will be sitting on the surface in front of you and your partner.

➢ Close your eyes, and go to the basic psychic level. Ask your partner to relax for a few minutes before the session begins. Each of you should imagine you are capable of easily transmitting information back and forth. Now open your eyes.

➢ The sender picks up the first card and begins sending the information from the card to the receiver. Take your time. Allow several minutes to pass as the receiver writes down what he or she believes is being received. The process continues until the sender has picked up each card and placed it facedown on the surface next to the original stack.

➢ Once you have gone through the entire deck of cards, compare what was on the cards to the notes taken by the receiver.

➢ Reverse rolls, and repeat the process. You can practice this as many times as you feel is possible during a sitting. I recommend you use this practice at least once per week in conjunction with the other ongoing practices until you feel comfortable with the outcome.

The next part of this process will involve the use of clairvoyance. Developing the ability to send information over a long distance generally occurs spontaneously. In the next practice, you will learn to transmit information over distance to a partner. Remember, each individual is unique. Some will have more of a propensity to send information while someone else will be a good receiver. As with all things you do, practice and focus can increase your ability. If this is part of your plan during this lifetime, you will master the technique. This practice may not interest you. If that is the case, determine why and move on.

Practice #2 Sending and Receiving Messages from Afar

➢ Identify your partner, and agree to a specific time for the encounter. Determine who will be the first sender and the time limitation for each person to be the sender and receiver. Each person will have a set of the cards you used earlier with scenery, people, animals, and so forth.

➢ At the designated time, go to your practice space, which is safe and free from internal and external distractions. Relax. Clear your mind of any thought about your day so that you can focus on the practice. When you feel completely relaxed, go to your basic psychic level. Begin transmitting. Remember to stack the cards in the order you send the information. When it is an individual's turn to receive information, be sure to document what comes through to you.

➢ At the end of the practice, compare your documentation to the image that was being transmitted on the card.

➢ I suggest you document the date and time of your practice sessions as well as what was transmitted and received.

Everything you learn through the practices will enhance your ability as a psychic. Undoubtedly, you will develop practice methods that will be your own and fashioned in a way to take you further down the psychic path, if you choose to do so. What I experience as a psychic medium requires the use of all of my psychic senses. The examples I use to illustrate what occurs for me definitely requires the use of telepathy.

CHAPTER 8

Out-of-body Experiences:
Astral Travel

One morning in March 2005 I awoke abruptly at 4:00 AM, feeling like I had just returned from a long journey and needed to rest. Suddenly, the face of a young woman I knew about through another relationship flashed in my mind. When I turned over in bed, I started recalling in detail a visit with this woman, who I will refer to as Vickie. The woman had been living in a semi comatose state for several years, and she was at the center of a controversy involving her family's decision to end her life. The family had decided to remove the woman's life support system, and they were emotionally distraught regarding the choice. As I recalled my visit with Vickie, I remembered entering the convalescent center where Vickie was being cared for. I floated over to her bedside and then hovered over her as she slept in her bed. As I looked at her face, she opened her eyes. My presence did not startle her, and she seemed to smile.

I then felt moved to ask Vickie, "Do you know you are going to die?" Following up, I said, "They have removed your life support."

Vickie seemed to become animated and responded to my question by saying, "No." Then she said to me, "I do not want to die. I need to tell someone."

Without any hesitation, she sat up in the bed, moved her feet over on to the floor, stood up, and started to walk out the door. As I floated next to her, she started walking down the hall. As I looked up, I saw a group of nurses and doctors walking in our direction and saying, "Vickie you must return to bed!" The next thing I could see was the group taking her by the arms and escorting her back to bed. I tried to speak to the medical team. However, only Vickie could hear or see me. As the team stood over her bed looking at her, I could hear Vickie trying to talk with the medical team, who seemed to ignore her.

I called out to the group, asking them to listen to the woman. I said, "Listen to her. She can speak!" My calls were to no avail, and the interaction ended. After I recounted the dream, I went back to sleep. The next morning at approximately 6:00 AM, I learned Vickie had died.

Astral projection or the out-of-body experience occurs spontaneously and occurs more often than we can imagine. The condition involves the physical body acting in a passive role while the "mind" or conscious is aware of what is happening. This ability to leave the physical body and explore this world and other worlds has great advantages. Sitting atop a mountain you have always wanted to climb or in the middle of the sea as the sun comes up, visiting the pyramids in Egypt, or walking through the jungles in Africa, it is all achievable. In many situations, you may go undetected by people wherever it is that you are visiting. However, you will also have the opportunity to converse with people you encounter and share information about your journeys if you choose. In addition to these possible adventures, if you decide to develop this skill, you will have opportunities to influence the material world during your travels in the astral realm.

We have discussed the subconscious mind in several of the practices you have completed so far. Let us regress for a moment and visit the definition of a human psyche or mind. The human psyche is described as conscious, subconscious, and unconscious. *Conscious* means being aware of all that is occurring in the material world. The unconscious state simply means you are not aware of the conscious state. One is unconscious during sleep, yet messages continue to be transmitted to the conscious mind during this state.

I am only going to introduce you to the concept of astral projection or the out-of-body experience. Because the process for developing this skill is quite complex, I will provide you with the basic practices necessary to begin your learning. While mastery of this skill requires many of the same techniques you have learned so far, the art is quite complex. It will require an entire new set of practices in addition to what you will learn here.

The first thing you must do will involve identifying the centers of activities in the body: crown center (white light of bright energy) located on the top of your head, brow center (light gray) located on your forehead, throat center (deep purple) located in the center of the throat, heart center (bright yellow) located in the region of your heart, sex center (circulating lavender) located in the area of your reproductive organs, and earth center (a swirling rainbow of bright colors) located at your feet.

To activate your centers, you must envision a shaft of the white light shining through your body and leaving you at the earth center. It then encircles the outside of your body and returns to your crown center to re-circulate. This energizing will allow you to activate a circle of energy that will ultimately serve as a psychic energy source. When your psychic substance is projected from the body, the circle of energy will assist you in pulling it back into the physical body when your travel is complete. It will also protect you against astral bleeding. The bleeding results from an excess of energy at the astral level that is out of control. By mastering the technique of circulating the energy evenly and consistently throughout and around your body, you achieve balance.

What is important to understand is that the complete astral body does not detach itself from the physical body during an out-of-body experience. The psyche for the astral body function remains to keep the heart beating, the brain on sleep mode, and the nervous system operating. While all of these functions do slow down during the projection, it is only to a certain point. A crucial issue with astral travel is that the individual must be focused. Understanding how to energize the body and ensure a complete re-entry occurs is important.

During the initial stages of development in astral projection, students are taught how to greet and love their lower self or the subconscious self, the mind or soul. You are asked to look closely at yourself in the mirror and learn to greet yourself each morning in a positive way that reinforces the fact that you love yourself. Through this ability to imagine yourself, just as you have learned to do in previous practices in this book, your ability to visualize will be important. You also will use your subconscious in a way that assists in the astral travel and re-entry.

The techniques for ejecting yourself start with establishing a safe place where you are free from internal and external interruptions. You will establish a regular time for each practice and keep the commitment to yourself. While there are several different postures used by those who teach astral projection, the one I am most familiar with and use is the Earth position. In this posture, you lay flat on the floor with your arms at your side. Your hands lay palm down. Your toes point down, away from the ceiling. Your back is as flat as possible while remaining comfortable. (For those individuals who have back problems, you may need to place a pillow beneath your legs). Remember to complete one practice per session. Repeat each practice one time per week until you are comfortable with the outcome.

Practice #1: Projection

➢ In your practice space, dim the lights. Make sure what you are wearing is comfortable. (Loose-fitting clothing is recommended.) Remove your eyeglasses and any other item that could be distracting. I always cover myself with a comforter because you can become quite cold during the projection.

➢ When you are comfortable, begin establishing a slowed rhythmic breathing to relax the body and allow concentration. As with each practice, astral projection will require you to be very relaxed. Inhale slowly, deeply through your nose. Hold the breath and then exhale through your mouth. Repeat this process at least seven times until you are comfortable. Close your eyes, and go to your basic psychic level.

➢ Speaking to yourself, say, "I am letting go of my fear of leaving my physical body." Create a vision of a cloudy substance floating above your physical body with a white line of energy connecting in through your stomach and up to the brilliant white light at the crown of your head. Now open your eyes and release the vision. Close your eyes as you continue to inhale in, hold the breath, and exhale. Realize you are becoming increasingly relaxed.

➢ Now you will energize each center of activity. As you inhale, hold your breath, and then exhale, imagine the brilliant white light sitting on the crown of your head. Feel the energy and strength it provides to your life force.

➢ Inhale, hold your breath, and exhale. Bring the brilliant light into the gray center located in the brow area of your head. Feel the energy and strength it provides your life force. Inhale, hold your breath, and exhale.

➢ Inhale, hold your breath, and exhale. Bring the brilliant white light into the purple throat area. Feel the energy and strength it provides your life force. As you inhale, hold your breath and exhale. Feel the connection between the crown of your head, the brow area of your face, and the throat. Inhale and exhale.

➢ Inhale, hold your breath, and exhale. Bring the brilliant white light into the yellow heart center located in your chest. Feel the energy and strength it provides your life force. As you inhale once more, feel the connection of the brilliant white light connected to your gray brow area, your purple throat area, and your yellow heart area as you gradually exhale.

➢ Inhale, hold your breath, and exhale. You are now drawing the brilliant white light from your yellow heart center into the lavender sexual organ center located in the abdomen and pelvic region of the body. Inhale, hold the breath, and exhale.

➢ Inhale and exhale as you feel the brilliant white light on the crown of your head pulsing through the brow center, into your throat center, into the heart and into your sex center. Inhale, hold and exhale.

➢ Inhale and exhale. Now, when you inhale, feel the brilliant white light flowing from your lavender sexual center in the abdomen into your rainbow-colored earth center surrounding your feet. As you breathe in and out, you will now feel the brilliant white light rushing up the outside of your body, outlining your legs, torso, arms, shoulders, neck, and face before reaching the crown center as it reconnects.

➢ Repeat the energizing exercise seven times before going on to the next step.

➢ When you are ready, with your eyes closed, say to your subconscious, "I am preparing my soul body to project into the astral realm for the purposes of spiritual evolution. I will let my subconscious know where I want to travel, who I want to see, and when I will return to my body."

➢ Inhale, hold the breath, and exhale. Imagine ejecting the substance of yourself as a white, fluffy mist connected to you in your abdomen region by the brilliant white light that can be used to pull the substance back into your body at any time. Cause the substance to form as an outline of your body. Do not see yourself or features in the substance. Allow the substance to be unique and neutral.

➢ You will now assign the traveler a task. Visualize the place or person you want to gain information about, cause the traveler to stand erect, and point them in the direction of the person or place. Let the traveler know the time they are to return. Visualize the traveler leaving the room, headed in the direction you have sent them to complete the task.

➢ Say to your subconscious, "That which is beneficial involving the traveler's experience will be easily recalled. I will see the experience vividly."

➢ Open your eyes. Resume your normal activities until it is time to reunite with the traveler.

➢ At the time of re-entry, enter your practice place, assume the earth position, and establish your rhythmic breathing.

➢ Go through the practice for energizing your centers of activity and continue inhaling, holding your breath, and exhaling.

➢ Now imagine you are calling the traveler back. Visualize it returning to the room and standing in front of you.

➢ Melt the traveler, and pull all of the substance back into your body through the brilliant white light in your abdomen.

➢ Inhale, hold your breath, and exhale. Ask your subconscious to bring the traveler's impressions to your conscious awareness.

➢ Keep a traveler's journal, and record the impression of each journey.

During the process of reuniting with the substance you eject, it is important to always put everything back in and keep your commitment to meet the traveler at the agreed-upon time. Performing this practice daily will help you in mastering the techniques of energizing your centers and in ejecting the traveler. What I have presented is a basic formula for you to utilize in learning the art of astral travel. If this is something you want to develop further, it will be important to intensify your study. I would suggest reading different books on the subject and listening to tapes.

While astral projection can occur spontaneously, when you intentionally attempt to achieve this state, it may not happen initially. The actual projection can take several practice sessions to accomplish. Do not be discouraged if you fall asleep during the first several practices or are not able to complete certain sections. In my own experience with astral travel I have found it necessary to be totally relaxed and free from all distractions. Clearing your mind and charging your body centers is crucial to the success of this process. When you do achieve ejection it will be obvious. You will "feel" the experience and see your soul substance.

Chapter 9

Problem Solving
and Your Psychic Ability

Daydreaming is a natural method most of us use to reenact life experiences. During this thinking process, we analyze what happened in particular scenario, what it could mean (whether good or bad), and how we responded or will need to respond in the future to have a particular or desired outcome. We create and rehearse our lines as well as interactions with others as if we are preparing for a great performance. Now imagine using what you have learned in terms of relaxation and visualization to influence your daydreaming experience and direct it in a focused manner to solve problems. At this stage of your development, you will now learn how to use the basic psychic ability to set and achieve goals.

Each of us has things in our life we want to achieve that will make us more successful, happy, or maybe just set free. It is certainly normal to want to learn new things in order to interact with people in such a way so that you fit in or any number of basic human desires that drive our thinking. While I strongly believe we come into this physical realm with a lesson plan and what we learn to do is directly related to that plan, it is also possible that an individual is directed to learn these psychic techniques in order to implement his or her plan. In essence, most of us have witnessed some people experiencing repeated success in most everything they do while other people with equal ability following the same plan fail. Part of the success or failure each of us experiences is a direct result of our life path and what we need to accomplish in order to reach a perfect state of knowledge. Therefore, I believe the closer we can come to understanding what we are intended to accomplish in this life can assist us in pursuing the right avenues more quickly.

Several things distinguish a successful from an unsuccessful person; however, when considering each situation, two points stand out for me. First, the successful person usually has a goal they are driven to accomplish versus the unsuccessful person who has not defined a goal. Second, the successful person takes the action to implement the goal while the unsuccessful person just daydreams about the possibility, waiting for the outcome to drop from the sky.

Just as each of us can develop our psychic abilities to a certain degree (depending on our commitment to mastery), each of us has the capability of identifying and implementing goals. At issue here is how we communicate with our mind, the subconscious, about what we want to achieve. Programming our mind with the information regarding our wishes is important. This life is full of people who would love to program your mind, such as business advertising the advantage of eating a burger versus a chicken sandwich or a peer lobbying you to do their job. Each will set goals for you if you do not take charge. By speaking with your mind at the basic psychic level and advising yourself about the wishes you have, you will initiate the process for making them come true. Just as you have advised your mind to develop your psychic ability, you can achieve other desires as well.

Let's begin this process at your basic psychic level in which you will create a chart listing your goals.

Practice #1: Goals and the Psychic Chart

➤ First, think about what it is you want to accomplish. (For me, as an example, it was to publish my first book by January 2005 on how I became a psychic medium, which I accomplished.)

➤ Select several sheets of white paper. (Printer paper will serve your purpose.) Mark the first five sheets as goal sheet one, goal sheet two, goal sheet three, goal sheet four, and goal sheet five. Place them in front of you in a stack, counting from one to five.

➤ On each piece of paper, write your goals separately. If you want a new car by a certain date, list the date, the model, the year, the color, and anything else that is specific associated with this goal. If you have a picture of the car, paste it onto the goal sheet so that you can specifically identify it during your psychic state. Continue to identify and describe your goals on the additional pages. If you do not have five goals, complete as many of the pages as you can.

➤ Read each goal several times until the image of your goal is clear in your mind.

➤ Go to your practice place that is safe and free from internal and external distractions. Make yourself comfortable, and place your goal sheets in front of you. Now that you are relaxed, go to your basic psychic level. Visualize goal number one.

➢ You will now state your specific goal to your subconscious, such as "I want to own this new car (state the specific model, color, and year) by (give the specific date)" or "I want to purchase a new home (visualize the home, color, style, and so forth) by (give the date)."

➢ Open your eyes, and think about your second goal. Once again, return to your basic psychic level. Repeat the process until you have stated each goal on your goal sheets.

➢ When you have described each goal for your subconscious, read the goals aloud. State to the wisdom of the universe that "Let no harm come to anyone because of the goals I wish to achieve."

➢ Place your goal sheets with your journals.

➢ The goals described on your goal sheets should be stated aloud each day for three months. You will review your goals in six months and, again, in one year. Remember to document what occurs and how you experience the implementation of the goals. Again, to make the message even more powerful, restate your goals each day. The art of mastery is in consistent practice.

When you notice the psychic mind guiding your path to facilitate opportunities to achieve, your goals document what is occurring. Often times, the interventions or directing is not observable. It is only after you have accomplished a goal that you will recognize an intervention.

Once you achieve the goals, go to your basic psychic level to give thanks. Remember, praise your inner self, and truly let yourself know it is loved. If a goal changes or you no longer have a desire to achieve a certain goal, just put a line through it, and say to yourself, "This is no longer a goal." You can add goals at any point; however, it is important to stay focused on your basic goals. If you change them often or repeat them in a different way when you state them to your psychic mind, it is confusing. Your mind will then turn off to the process. Make the goal sheet your own. Once a goal is achieved, if you want to do so, add another one.

You should see some type of action directing you toward achieving your goals within the first three months. While this process is a method for directing your life, you will need to participate beyond just creating the goal sheet and directing you psychic mind. Because we are all connected to the universe, miracles and occurrences that would be called supernatural do occur. However, we still must invest some part of ourselves in order to accomplish our goals.

I go to my basic psychic level every day and restate my goals. In the evening, when I have downtime, I take a few minutes to once again return to my basic psychic level and state my goals. My psychic mind has a clear picture of what my goals are, and I experience the influence provided by the higher universal intelligence and my psychic mind daily.

Focusing your energy and programming your own life direction is a positive step toward understanding your mission in this lifetime. If you were not clear before beginning this learning process about what you need to do in this lifetime, there is a chance you will determine this during the goal sheet process.

Next, you will learn a deeper technique for identifying what you are intended to accomplish in this lifetime. Developing a relationship with your guardian angel, spirit mentor, and spirit guide is key to discovering who you are and your mission for this lifetime.

When I made a firm commitment to utilize my gift and become a professional psychic medium, before I embarked upon the endeavor, I utilized meditation more frequently. Because of this focus, I met my guardian angel. He told me his name and affirmed his name by leading me to a restaurant where I had never been before with his name. I had never passed by this very old establishment nor had I ever visited the section of town where it was located. Each time I would converse with my guardian, he would share a new piece of information regarding an individual or situation in life that was about to occur. He forewarned me of my sister's death and provided the date, month, and year it would happen. However, long before he started to provide me with prophetic information, he asked me to channel communications for the spiritual realm. After accepting this opportunity, I was bombarded by spiritual visitations and communications. I knew I was being directed to utilize my psychic abilities professionally. Certainly, to question the guidance would have involved denying why I came into this life in the first place. During this time, I was also directed to two different psychics who acknowledged my extraordinary skills immediately upon meeting me and asked me when I would begin to practice. The spiritual realm, the angelic realm, and people in the physical world who supported the direction I was receiving from the other side motivated me to pursue the correct path. Finally, an acquaintance, who has become a dear friend, unexpectedly started to ask me questions about my psychic skills. This inquiry was the spark that ignited my professional practice and helped me to succeed in my intended work. In conjunction with establishing my practice, the opportunity came up for me to write my first book, *Impressions: Communicating with Spirits a Psychic Medium's Perspective*, which described my life experiences as a developing medium.

When I first became aware of my guardian angel, I only heard messages in my own voice tone. In some instances, the communication was direct and clear. Still, there were times when I had to decipher the information that came through and piece together the message. I was always curious about the other side, his appearance, and things that did not hold a meaning for those existing in the spiritual realm. Often, I was redirected to what I needed to accomplish, particularly if I was preparing for a reading and became sidetracked. Then, during a visualization practice, I asked my guardian angel and spirit guide to join me in the life meadow where time and space do not limit our travels. I was surprised as both walked up and took a position on my left and right. My guardian angel then sat down beside me on my right side, and my spirit guide continued to stand to my left side. I was delighted by the encounter. I continue to visit with both in the same spot in the meadow when I am seeking wisdom on a variety of subjects.

Perhaps you are curious about the life meadow and how it is used. First, the life meadow is a place that is not constrained by the boundaries of time or space. In this psychic space, the rules of the physical world do not apply. As you travel psychically, you will use this place in the meadow to enter the past and the future. This meadow is different from the basic psychic level you experience in the mind. It goes much deeper and helps you in accomplishing the psychic missions you will create or take on. The next practice will help you reach the meadow and use it appropriately.

Practice #2: The Meadow of Time

➢ Go to your practice space where you are safe and free from internal and external distractions. Settle into your comfortable position or posture. Begin breathing in and out. Imagine you are relaxing and focusing your energy in order to take a peaceful journey. Close your eyes, and breathe in. This time, as you breathe out, say to your subconscious, "I am releasing all of the issues of this day into the universe. I am focusing my attention on my journey." Open your eyes. Continue to breathe in and out.

➢ Close your eyes again, knowing you are relaxed and free from distractions. Go to your basic psychic level.

➢ Say to your subconscious, "I am going to the meadow of time by counting five, four, three, two, and one. As I say one, I am stepping onto the grass in the meadow of time." Visualize yourself standing in a meadow full of flowers. This place is so peaceful, so quiet, and calm. The meadow stretches to the right and to the left. In front of you is the deep blue sky sitting atop a thin line of earth. The sky is the awareness of the universe, the consciousness that connects everything and everyone. You are standing on a path in the current time.

➢ Enjoy the beauty, touch the grass, and smell the sweet scent of the flowers. Know you are safe here in this place of all knowing and love. You are relaxed.

➢ Look slowly to the right. Note a thicket of trees preventing you from seeing past a certain point. This is where all things past exist.

➤ Look to your left, and note a thicket of trees preventing you from seeing past a certain point. This is where all things in the future exist.

➤ Say to yourself, "I can return to the meadow of time any time I choose just by going to my basic psychic level and counting down from five, four, three, two, and one."

➤ Now count from one to five as the meadow of time disappears.

➤ Open your eyes.

This practice is a major component in helping you attain a psychic state to use at will. Practice it as often as possible in your safe space. You will reach a point where you can use this ability with your eyes open and anywhere you choose.

Practice #3: The Past

➤ Go to your safe place where you are free from internal and external interruptions. Begin breathing in and out. Slowly relax. Become comfortable in your position or posture. Close your eyes for a moment, and say to yourself, "I am free from the activities of the day, and my subconscious focuses on this journey."

➤ Close your eyes as you breathe in and out. Go to your basic psychic level.

➤ Imagine yourself about to enter the meadow of time. Slowly begin to count down from five to one.

➤ You are in the meadow of time. Take a moment. Look to the right, and see the thicket of trees. State to your subconscious the date, time, and place you want to be transported. Begin to walk into the thicket of trees. When you arrive at the end of the thicket, you will be standing at the edge of the place you desire to be. Go forward, and examine where you are. Talk with people. See if you recognize anyone. When you are ready to return to present time, say to your subconscious, "I am ready to return to the present." Turn, and look behind you. You will automatically see the thicket. Walk into the thicket. You will then walk into the meadow of time.

➢ When you are ready to return to your safe place, count from one to five. Open your eyes.

➢ You will complete the same process for going into the future except you will enter to your left. Remember to be specific about the date, time, and place you wish to visit.

Whatever period you need to do work in can be done in the meadow of time. This is a place where you can also identify your guardian angel, spirit guide, or spirit mentor. Thereafter, invite your guardian angel to watch over you in your daily life and as you travel in the meadow of time. Each time you take a journey into the past or future ask him or her to alert you to return to the current time and make sure you are responsive.

When you choose to do work in the current time, just remain in the meadow of time. State where you want to be. You will find yourself transported to the exact time and place where you desire. Remember to always let your psychic mind know you appreciate everything it does for you. When you go to the place you desire, remember to keep a journal of your travels and record the outcomes. Acknowledge your psychic mind by saying, "I am a spiritual being able to transcend the physical body and travel through the universe existing beyond time and space." Begin to acknowledge inner self in this way just before you take a journey.

As you can see, the practices are becoming increasingly more complex and taking you to a deeper level of psychic consciousness. The meadow of time—present, past, and future—can now be accessed at any time. You can use the meadow of time to do your practices in lieu of the basic psychic level. This state is powerful and potentially more affective with practice than completing your work at the basic psychic level. Before conducting a group session, it is this level I use to complete my meditations to call upon those who have passed over to join me. In this state, I ask those who have passed over to talk with me, identify themselves, and provide me with messages for members of their family or friends who will be attending the session. Often, those who have passed over will step through a bright white light so I can see their features, clothing, and mannerisms. I will also hear pieces of information about a loved one or something about the deceased that can be used during a session. Additionally, I will pick up names, interests, fragrances, or emotions relating to a person on this side or who has passed over.

I utilize meditation as a means to focus my attention on those who have passed over. The art of meditation is a valuable tool for those who engage in psychic work and can be completed from the meadow of time. I enjoy lying in a comfortable position with my down comforter pulled gently over my body so I can move freely. For me, I find peace in practicing or meditating in a dark room with a candle and the light fragrance of my favorite incense. (Remember to make sure the candle is in a safe, secure place in the room. Also, it is good to burn the incense just before you enter the room so the air is clean and only the scent remains.)

Meditating is quite simple; however; you must relax and allow all of the distractions you have encountered during the day to dissipate. You will go to your practice space where you are free from internal and external distractions. When you have prepared your space in a way that makes you feel comfortable, you will lie on the floor with your head situated comfortably. Your arms and legs will be lying straight down from the body. Now is the time to remember what you have learned regarding how to prepare for astral travel. Energizing you body centers is empowering and enhances your psychic awareness. Think about the white light as it flows through your body and touches each center.

Practice #4: The Art of Meditation

➤ You are comfortably situated in your practice place. Close your eyes, and begin breathing in and out. Breathe in, and breathe out. Concentrate on your breathing, and feel the gentle relaxation of the healing air as you take it in through your nose. Breathe out through your mouth, releasing all of the toxins from the external world and those you have stored in your body. Repeat this breathing, saying, "As I breathe in the healing air, I become more and more relaxed. As I breathe out, I release all of the toxins taken in during the day and am relaxed."

➤ Open your eyes, and close your eyes. Count backwards from five to one. Know you have arrived in the meadow of time. See yourself setting on the grass and relaxing. Say to your subconscious, "My mind is open to receive the energy, information, and guidance from the universal consciousness."

➤ At this time, you can ask a deceased loved one to join you just by inviting them to sit next to you in the meadow. If they join you, remember to ask them questions and thank them for speaking with you or joining you. At this time, you can send positive, healing messages to a loved one or friend. At this time your could ask for guidance from spiritual mentors or guardian angels.

➤ How you choose to use you meditation is up to you. When you have finished the meditation and want to return to the present, simply say, "I am ready to return." Begin counting from one to five. Open your eyes. Once again, remember to record what has occurred.

Decide to complete the meditations daily, if possible. This is an expansion of your practice at the basic psychic level. Anything you practice or did at the basic psychic level can now be completed in the meadow of time. While it takes more time, it is extremely focused and ultimately more beneficial. Still, there are times when you need information or assistance immediately, and the basic psychic level will work in this situation. When you are in a position that does not allow you to close your eyes, the basic psychic level will work.

In order to allow your mind and the universal consciousness to respond, it is to your advantage to stay focused on one practice at a time. Once you have completed a practice or meditation, you can begin the next. However, if you are problem solving, sending a psychic healing, or focusing on a specific situation in the present, future, or past, only complete one travel during a session. If you override your psychic mind or the universal consciousness with too many tasks or questions, you can cancel out the process. Just like when you set your goals and program your psychic consciousness, it is important to stay focused on those goals in order to see them through to accomplishment. It is also important to focus your attention on specific task or questions when completing the practices you have learned.

Practice #5: How Can I Use My Abilities?

➤ Go to your practice place where it is safe from internal and external distractions. Close your eyes, and breathe in and out until you feel relaxed and free from the stresses of the day. Open your eyes. Close your eyes, and count from five to one as you find yourself standing in the meadow of time.

➤ Walk into the meadow of flowers, and feel the warm, soft grass beneath your feet. Touch the flowers that are circling your waist. As the gentle sun pours down over your body, feel how soft and warm the flowers are. This helps you feel relaxed and at peace.

➤ Ask the universal consciousness, "What is my path for using my psychic abilities?"

➤ As you stand or sit there on the grass, ask other questions relating specifically to your psychic abilities. You can remain here as long as you care to remain. You are safe.

➤ When you are ready to return from the meadow of time, count from one to five. Open your eyes. Document your experience and what you discovered on this journey.

Practice #6: Seeking Help or Advice

➤ Go to your practice space where you are safe from internal and external distractions. Relax, and clear your mind of any thought about your day so that you can focus on the practice. When you feel completely relaxed, go to your basic psychic level. Close your eyes, and count from five to one. Arrive in the meadow of time.

➤ You will know what you need help with, and will be prepared to ask your spirit guide or guardian angel a specific question.

➤ Now, ask your spirit guide and/or guardian angel to come join you in the meadow. When he or she has joined you ask your question. You may receive an immediate response from your spirit guide or guardian angel. However, your response may come to you from the outside world and may not occur immediately.

➤ When you are done, regardless of what occurs, acknowledge your spirit guide and/or guardian angel. Thank them for helping you.

➤ When you are ready to leave, count from one to five. Find yourself opening your eyes. Document what occurred in your journal.

Practice #7: Problem Exploration and Solutions

➤ Go to your practice space that is free from internal and external distractions. Relax, and clear your mind of any thought about your day so that you can focus on the practice. When you feel completely relaxed, go to your basic psychic level. Begin breathing in the healing air and expelling the toxins you may have collected until you are comfortable with your space. Open your eyes.

➤ Once again, return to your basic psychic level or the meadow of time. If there is a situation that you do not want in your life, visualize what you see that bothers you.

➢ Begin to dissect the situation, and look at all of the nuances. Say to yourself, "I do not want this in my life!"

➢ Just as you were able to erase your name from the square you drew, erase the picture, and replace it with exactly what you want.

➢ Look at the new picture with as much intensity as you did the unwanted situation. Say to yourself with great joy, "This is what I want!"

➢ Then say, "I release this matter to the universal intelligence and my subconscious."

➢ Count from one to five. Open your eyes, and arrive in the present.

Use this method at any time to re-create scenarios or situations that require immediate attention and dispel negative energy. Your shield is a good defense against negative influence or energy entering your life. However, circumstances will occasionally arise that require immediate attention so that you can move on emotionally and feel as though the problem is successfully solved. This is an excellent way to immediately release yourself from emotional distress and allow your subconscious to solve the problem. I have used this technique when dealing with individuals who think differently from me and insist I need to do what they want me to do. For example, a relative once attempted to persuade me not to pursue a Master's degree. They were disturbed with my pursuits and attempted to convince me that completing another degree was of no value. While I certainly did not believe what the individual was saying, it was painful to experience someone I cared for in such distress over something that was none of his or her concern. I decided that I needed to re-create the relationship through a psychic visualization. I went into the meadow to time and erased the negative behavior. I then created a scenario where the individual was happy and had activities to engage in that were fulfilling. The following month I learned that the relative was taking care of his grandchildren and shuttling them between appointments. He was providing a service for the parents of the children that made him happy and kept him busy. The person has never attempted to use aggressive communication with me again and our relationship is friendly. The results of the positive visualization were amazing and all of the negative energy disappeared.

The psychic work you will complete in the future will involve asking your spirit guide, guardian angel, or spirit mentor for advice or help. It is important to become comfortable with going to the meadow of time. It is also important to ask them to join you and assist you in whatever psychic endeavor you are pursuing or issues you have in general.

Your spiritual guide, mentor, and guardian angel are here to assist you through your journey in life. Do not hesitate to call upon them for help or guidance. However, always remember to acknowledge their help and to thank them.

CHAPTER 10

Psychic Communication and the Other Side

I have experienced my gift as a psychic medium since the age of five. Several members of my family, including my father, had ongoing experiences with the spiritual realm. I grew up considering these encounters natural. I was never uncomfortable with what society thought to be strange or supernatural. The other side has used the sense of smell, touch, psychic communication, clairvoyance, and materialization to get my attention. My first memory of an encounter involved three spirits who materialized at night. They walked over to my bed and said my name. The house was full of energy, and I was not the only one who was visited at night.

Not everyone will have an interest in communicating or interacting in some way with spiritual entities. If you do, you can use your psychic ability to make contact. In fact, you will be able to visit with any deceased individual who chooses to communicate with this side by inviting him or her to come into your awareness and make contact.

As with me, the contacts will not just involve a mental contact. At times, you will experience many different sensations and possibly the materialization of the visiting party. In order to make contact with a deceased party, angel, entity, or spirit guide, go to the meadow of time.

Practice #1: Contact

➤ Go to your practice place that is safe from internal and external distractions. Breathe in and out until you feel you are focused and all of the day's distractions have disappeared. Close your eyes. Then open them.

➤ Close your eyes, and count from five to one. You will find yourself standing in the meadow of time. In front of you, there is a brilliant white light and an open door. Say, "If there is anyone on the other side who would like to speak to me, please come forward."

➤ Focus on the light, and allow this to happen naturally. Listen for information, names, songs, smells, and so forth. Continue to focus on the light. If no one walks through immediately, ask again, "Is there is anyone on the other side who would like to communicate with me, I am available." (Do not be disappointed if you do not have a response the first time you try. Just like every practice you have learned, this one will take time as well.)

➤ If someone walks through immediately, thank him or her for coming forward. Ask him or her if he or she has something to say to you. If they do not respond immediately, ask questions like "How are you?" If you do not recognize the spirit, ask, "What is your name?" When you receive a response, be sure to thank him or her for talking with you.

If the spirit does not respond at all, simply thank him or her for making contact. Invite him or her to contact you again. Thank the spirit for coming.

➢ When you are ready to leave, say, "I am saying good-bye for now, but I will return. Thank you for coming through to me. My love is with you. Let me know when you are near if you visit again." Count from one to five. Find yourself opening your eyes.

I have developed a specific visualization that I use during my meditations to make contact with the spiritual realm just before a reading. You can also develop a specific method for making contact. At this stage of the practices, creating different scenery or other visualizations methods is possible.

When you pursue contact with the other side, do not be afraid of their world or the encounters. The other side has its priorities, and those who come forward to share information with the living do so in an effort to provide comfort. If you feel uncomfortable with contact, remember you have created a brilliant white shield of light that protects you. You are in control and can always return to your safe place. Enjoy your experiences and the gift you are utilizing.

Practice #2: Physical Healing

➢ Go to your safe place that is free from internal and external distractions. Begin breathing in and out until you feel completely relaxed. Close your eyes for a moment and then open them.

➢ Close your eyes, and go to the meadow of time by counting from five to one. Once again, you will find yourself standing in the meadow of flowers.

> You are going to use your ability to visualize anything or anyone at any time, accompanied by your ability to create anything you want at any time you want. In your deep psychic state of consciousness, look at what area of the body requires healing.

> Systematically begin to examine your head, throat, chest, stomach, legs and feet. Imagine that you are now going inside your body to examine your brain, heart, lungs, stomach, intestines, muscle tissue veins and blood. If you see or sense in abnormalities you are going to create a psychic patch that will heal that area. For example, perhaps you have a wound that needs to heal. Visualize a patch of skin that you will use to cover the wound. Written on the top of the skin are the words healing patch. Now imagine applying the patch to the wound. Each time you see or sense that something in your body requires repair then create the healing patch and apply it to the area.

> When you have applied the healing patch to those parts of the body that need some repair declare to your subconscious that you are completely healthy. Let your subconscious know that if you require a repair in the future you will ask for healing services to be administered. Thank your subconscious for the healing.

> When you are ready to return, you will count from one to five. Open your eyes, and return to the present.

On one occasion, when I was living alone, I developed a severe case of flu accompanied by bronchitis. It was very late at night and my fever was quite high. I decided to go to a deep psychic level in the meadow of time and attempt a healing. I visualized me entering my body and systematically pushing all of the infection and virus to the surface of my skin where it would be dispelled into the universe. After two hours of meditation, my fever broke. I was then able to sleep for the next two hours. When I woke up in the morning, my chest and back was covered with a red rash. However, the bronchitis and fever seemed to be gone. I scheduled an appointment with my physician, who informed me there was no reason for the rash and confirmed that the bronchitis was gone. I explained to her what I had done during the night in an attempt to push the virus and infection from my body. Because she believed in the possibility of an individual possessing the ability to heal his or her body, she suggested the rash might be the result of my actions. The following morning, the rash was gone completely. I then went running. I knew, with a tremendous amount of focus during a meditation and by asking my guardian angel to assist me, I could direct my body to heal. I have since engaged in various meditations to cause healing to occur, and I have been successful.

During your use of the various practices, you will be able to go to your basic psychic level or the meadow of life and engage your subconscious as well as guardian angel in most any of the endeavors you wish to pursue. The important thing is focusing and identifying what you are attempting to do when you decide to engage in an activity. You can pursue the solving of personal problems or issues others are having, identifying your career path, determining how you are intended to use your psychic gift, and many other things we have discussed so far. Be assertive in your psychic pursuits, and be clear about what you want to accomplish. In the initial practices, remember you learned to release feathers, draw on a board, and erase it all in an attempt to help you develop your visualization capabilities within your subconscious. The better you are at bringing the picture forth in your mind with great detail, the easier it is for the subconscious to understand what you are attempting to accomplish. In addition, how you state a problem or ask a question should be specific. If you repeat it more than once, you should be consistent in stating the problem, question, or goals.

CHAPTER 11

Developing Your Danger Signal

You now know your subconscious mind has the ability to do many things; including letting you know when danger is near. One morning, when my husband was leaving for a long day trip, I desperately wanted to accompany him on the journey. We had already discussed the fact it was not possible for me to take the trip because of a commitment out of my control, but I woke up that morning and felt a sense of desperation in needing to accompany him. I questioned him repeatedly about going with him. He consistently attempted to console me by saying he would be home by 6:00 that evening. Finally, I stalled him for a few more minutes until I could get my camera and take his picture.

As the day went on, I started to feel increasingly disconnected from my husband. I knew something was going on, and I could not decide what was occurring. By 4:30 that afternoon, I decided to drive to the local store and buy a few things for dinner, just to get my mind off what I was feeling. When I arrived home at 5:00, there was a message on the answering machine from a hospital in the town where my husband's meeting had occurred. I immediately called the hospital and learned my husband had been involved in a near-fatal car accident. I rushed to his side in the hospital, where they had decided to hold him for observation overnight. The next day, when I checked him out of the hospital, we drove by the wrecking yard so that I could see the car and get some of his belongings from the vehicle. The roof of the car was caved in, and I learned the Jaws of Life had been used to free him. After being struck by the airbag, he was knocked unconscious and slumped over in the seat. Because he was hunched over against the door, he escaped being crushed. I had wanted to go with him because I had sensed an impending danger. Perhaps the accident could have been avoided if I had gone because we would have stayed for dinner or I might have been killed in the accident.

My guardian angel has protected me in so many different circumstances that include life-threatening circumstances as well as situations that could have disrupted my life. To activate your system, you will go to the meadow of life and make contact with your guardian angel or spirit guide. When you have asked him or her to join you, ask that he or she alert you to dangers and situations that will be disruptive to your well-being. Decide how he or she will get your attention. My guardian angel will use extraordinary means to alert me to danger. For example, he will cause the garage door to simply not open. (This has happened twice. In both circumstances, I would have been in grave danger had he not stalled me.) In other situations, I receive the direct message and know what is going to happen. For instance, with our rental house, I knew when an appliance was going out and in what month. I was shown the appliance and directed to purchase a replacement. In other situations, I knew when a renter was going to move and would be alerted by an overwhelming need to place an ad in the newspaper advertising the unit for rent. The list is infinite. Therefore, my guardian angel is direct in communicating with me about danger and life situations that will cause distress. However, you might ask your guardian to flash a sign in your mind or provide a special word that causes you to listen more carefully to information coming through in order to alert you to matters of concern.

Practice #1: Setting Up the Alarm

> ➤ Go to your practice place where you are safe from internal and external distractions. Take your favorite position, and begin breathing in and out. Advise your mind that, as you breathe out, all of the tension from the day dissipates into the universe. As you breathe in again, advise your mind that you are breathing in the healing air of the universe. Feel yourself beginning to relax. Close your eyes for a few moments. Then open them.

> ➤ Close your eyes, and begin counting from five to one. Arrive in the meadow of time. Ask your guardian angel to join you in the meadow.

> ➤ Let your guardian angel know you want to be warned of dangers that will harm you or others and situations that will cause you distress. Identify a method to let you know you are in danger, (for example, your guardian angel could flash a red stop sign repeatedly in your mind). Let your guardian know this will be the signal for you to listen for his or her message if he or she needs your attention.

> ➤ Thank your guardian angel for joining you and for alerting you in the future of potential dangers.

> When you are ready to leave, count from one to five. Find yourself in the present.

Each day, when you wake up, remind your guardian angel to warn you of dangers. For your own comfort, you might want to restate the signal for the first month as a reminder. You will never need to reprogram this warning system. This message will last throughout your life. All you need to do is listen.

CHAPTER 12

General Exercises to Sharpen Your Skills

Each day you complete the practices, you will increase your psychic ability. Mastery of technique involves repetition, concentration, focus, and a commitment to improve. While I did not have any formal training as a child, everything that has been described in each practice I experienced naturally, and I used these skills at all times. For those who are embarking upon this learning journey, know the basic skills will become natural to you in time. I have built upon my skills since childhood. If you choose to take your learning beyond this book, you will also find yourself improving with time and practice.

Now may be the time for you to become creative and design your own techniques or practices. You now understand each technique for achieving different psychic states and the reasons behind learning each. I would suggest taking the feather exercise and adapting it so that you create another object (using the same colors) drifting into the clouds. Create something you will identify with, for example, a round piece of colored wood, a balloon, a piece of string, or whatever you can imagine.

Practice #1: Creating Your Own Practices

➤ Go to your practice space where you are safe from internal and external distractions. Take a position in the space that is comfortable for you, and begin breathing in and out. Recognize, with each breath out, the toxins of the environment are leaving your body. As you breathe in, a healing energy comes over your entire body. Relax, and close your eyes.

➤ Open your eyes.

➤ Close your eyes, and go to your basic psychic level. Imagine, for example, holding a red, orange, yellow, green, light blue, sapphire blue, and lavender string all blowing lightly upwards toward the sky.

➤ Release the red string. Watch it as it disappears into the clouds. Release the orange string. Watch it drift into the clouds, disappearing from view. Then watch the yellow string, the green string, the light blue string, the sapphire blue string, and the lavender string. All float gently out of view, disappearing into the clouds and the universal intelligence.

➤ Open your eyes. You have just created your own version of a visualization practice and can adapt many of the practices to fit your desire.

Try adapting other practices in the same manner. For example, with the vertical visualization exercise, I use a large ball of colored concrete. I personally roll it from the right side of my vision to the left and then back again. By using the heavy object, I am able to see the entire object roll across my vision in the mind without much effort. I can practice at any time.

We only briefly touched on the subject of psychic healing. Even the mere mention of the possibility for me is chilling. This involves a tremendous amount of commitment and accountability. As with all things in the universe, one must remember there is an intelligent energy far greater than any-one who attempts to intervene in the lives of mortals. In addi-tion, I personally believe, as I have stated previously in the book, we each come into this life with a mission to accom-plish. While a healing may be part of our life plan, it also may not be part of that plan. The psychic healer must be aware of the universal power when attempting this process and under-stand he or she cannot interfere with an individual's destiny. However, if you decide to develop this skill, your best approach, as with all of the practices, is to go forward with confidence, focusing on your goal and have faith. Prayer is a form of psychic healing, even though some within the church would disagree. Bringing forth the brilliant white light of energy and pushing it through to your hands to lay upon someone who is sick can produce healing affects. You can also visualize healing someone from afar. Healing, however, is the result of God's energy focused through the messenger. It is not the individual psychic who possesses this power to heal or complete any other psychic work. When you engage in a heal-ing activity, you become an instrument to channel God's healing energies to the individual requiring this blessing.

Again, understanding that psychics are not physicians, one should never encourage an individual to utilize your service in lieu of seeking medical advice. This profession does not lend itself to ego. The individual who is practicing as a psychic must always be humble and work with the universal intelligence, not attempt to compete with the greater power.

Practice #2: Look Inside Your Physical Body

➤ First, find a diagram of the human body that has illustrations of the internal and external structure as well as organs. Study this material carefully so that you can see a picture of everything with your mind's eye through visualization.

➤ Go to your practice place that is free of internal and external distractions. Establish your position, and become comfortable. Through breathing, let go of all of the activities that occurred during the day. Allow the healing air of the universal consciousness to enter your body. Close your eyes. Then open them.

➤ Close your eyes, and count from five to one. Find yourself in the meadow of time present.

➤ Bring forth the vision of your body into your psychic mind. You are now going to look inside your body and examine all of your organs, including the brain, eyes, sinuses, throat, heart, lungs, liver, pancreas, stomach, intestines, sex organs, blood vessels, skeletal structure, and muscles in great detail.

➤ Take as much time as you need because this is your body. You want to become acquainted with all of it, including the blood flowing through your veins.

➤ If you see or sense that something is not right in an area of your body, fix the problem. Imagine a healing spray emitted from a machine moving slowly through the body. When the spray touches the problem area healing occurs.

Perhaps you will need a vacuum cleaner and a sponge that is filled with self-healing fluid. Clean the problem area. Then apply the healing fluid. Imagine whatever you need to imagine in order to correct the problem.

➤ When you have finished the examination, say to your subconscious mind, "I am finished now and I am healthy." Let you subconscious know that should you require healing in the future you will ask for the healing services.

➤ Open your eyes.

Psychic healing is a fragile, yet powerful, gift. The individual who chooses to use this gift can do it with a person they are able to touch or from afar. Because we are each a part of this beautiful loving universe, send love and healing as often as you can to individuals and the earth. When you see a person in distress on the street, in the media, or someone pops into your mind, send them love and healing. As part of any ritual you develop to enhance your psychic abilities, make sending love and healing out into the universe a part of this process.

Practice #3: The Art of Relaxation

➤ Go to your place of practice that is free of distractions and find your position. Close your eyes, and allow your whole body to relax. Feel safe as you breathe in healing air and exhale any toxins from the day.

➤ Begin to notice how calm you are feeling and how the deep breaths you are taking relax you increasingly.

➤ Say to your subconscious, "I am going to relax." Begin counting from ten to one as you find yourself becoming increasingly more relaxed. Say to yourself, "I will become quite relaxed, free from worry, and alert yet comfortable, knowing my guardian angel will make me aware of any emergencies."

➤ At ten, relax your hands and forearms, allowing the tension to flow first through your right hand and exiting out the fingertips as a brilliant white light flows into its place. Then feel the tension flowing from your left forearm out through the tips of your fingers on the left hand, which is followed by the healing brilliant white light.

➤ At nine, let the brilliant white light flow into your upper arms, pushing the tensions away as the healing flows into your biceps and triceps. Say to yourself, "I feel good, relaxed, and happy."

➤ At eight, your shoulders and neck are completely relaxed as the brilliant white light of healing bathes them and relaxes the tension.

➤ At seven, the brilliant white light that sits on the crown of your head is glowing as it sends the healing light to all parts of your body. The top of your head, forehead and eyes, cheeks, lips, and jaw are all relaxed and pulsing with the healing energy of the brilliant white light.

➤ At six, you are relaxing more and more as the energy continues to proceed down your body.

➤ At five, your lungs, upper back, and chest are releasing the tension as the brilliant white light flows in to heal and relax you.

➤ At four, your stomach is completely relaxed. There is no tension or discomfort in the area that is filled with the white light of healing. Your lower back is relaxed as the white light pulses through your spine and heals all of the area, releasing the tension.

➤ At three, the muscles in your arms and legs are completely relaxed.

➤ At two, the brilliant white, pulsing light is surrounding your body and moves into your calves, feet, and toes. It exits your body through the toes and comes back up to the top of your head.

➤ At one, you are totally relaxed all over. All of the tension is gone from your body, and the healing white light surrounds you with healing energy and protection. You are calm and happy.

➤ Say to yourself, "I can create any image, creature, or vision I choose. I control my journeys and remember everything in detail that occurs during my experience.

➤ When you are ready to return to the present, begin counting from one to ten. Open your eyes. Find yourself completely awake and in your safe place.

Practice #3 can be used to reduce stress. Just as you created the aura of white light to shield you from negative energy or forces, you can say to yourself during the session, "No demands or pressure from outside influences will enter my psychic mind. I am shielded from all tension and stress. I feel calm and relaxed throughout the day. If I need protection, I need the white shield of energy to be up, and I will be protected. All of the bad or negative energy will bounce off my shield and dissipate into the universe, causing no harm to anyone."

Practice #4: Reduction of Pain

➤ Go to your place of practice that is free of distractions, and find your position. Close your eyes, and allow your whole body to relax. Feel safe as you breathe in healing air and exhale any toxins from the day.

➤ Begin to notice how calm you are feeling and how the deep breaths you are taking relax you increasingly.

➤ Say to your subconscious, "I am going to relax." Begin counting from ten to one as you find yourself becoming increasingly more relaxed, saying to yourself, "I will become quite relaxed, free from worry, and alert yet comfortable. I know my guardian angel will make me aware of any emergencies."

➤ At ten, relax your hands and forearms, allowing the tension to flow first through your right hand and exit out the fingertips as a brilliant white light flows into its place. Then feel the tension flowing from your left forearm out through the tips of your fingers on the left hand, which is followed by the healing brilliant white light.

➤ At nine, let the brilliant white light flow into your upper arms, pushing the tensions away as the healing flows into your biceps and triceps. Say to yourself, "I feel good, relaxed, and happy."

➤ At eight, your shoulders and neck are completely relaxed as the brilliant white light of healing bathes them and relaxes the tension.

➤ At seven, the brilliant white light that sits on the crown of your head is glowing as it sends the healing light to all parts of your body. The top of your head, forehead and eyes, cheeks, lips, and jaw are all relaxed and pulsing with the healing energy of the brilliant white light.

➢ At six, you are relaxing more and more as the energy continues to proceed down your body.

➢ Five, my lungs, upper back and chest are releasing the tension as the brilliant white light flows into to heal and relax me.

➢ At four, your stomach is completely relaxed. There is no tension or discomfort in the area that is filled with the white light of healing. Your lower back is relaxed as the white light pulses through your spine and heals all of the area, releasing the tension.

➢ At three, the muscles in your arms and legs are completely relaxed

➢ At two, the brilliant white, pulsing light is surrounding your body and moves into your calves, feet, and toes. It exits your body through the toes and comes back up to the top of your head.

➢ At one, you are totally relaxed all over. All of the tension is gone from your body, and the healing white light surrounds you with healing energy and protection. You are calm and happy.

➢ Say to yourself, "I can create any image, creature, or vision I choose. I control my journeys and remember everything in detail that occurs during the experience."

➢ Imagine your pain can be moved and escorted out of the body. Feel the spot where you are experiencing the pain. Move it around, and know you can push it out of your body.

➢ Say to yourself, "I am completely relaxed, but I am choosing to feel my pain so I can describe it to my psychic mind." Now feel the pain, and visualize moving the pain from it current location all the way down to the tip of your toes where the brilliant white, healing light rushes in to push it out of your body and heal the area. Continue moving any pain you are experiencing out of your body until it is completely gone. Feel the brilliant white light rushing through your body and healing any area where there was distress.

➢ When you are ready to return to the present, begin counting from one to ten. Open your eyes, and find yourself completely awake and in your safe place.

As your skills evolve, you will want to challenge yourself by trying new techniques and, once again, creating your own. The premise for most practices is the same; however, use your imagination as you grow in this gift.

Practice #5: Self-Strength, Building Confidence

➢ Go to your place of practice that is free of distractions and find your position. Close your eyes, and allow your whole body to relax. Feel safe as you breathe in healing air and exhale any toxins from the day.

➢ Begin to notice how calm you are feeling and how the deep breaths you are taking relax you increasingly.

➢ Say to your subconscious, "I am going to relax." Begin counting from ten to one as you find yourself becoming increasingly more relaxed. Say to yourself, "I will become quite relaxed, free from worry, and alert yet comfortable. I know my guardian angel will make me aware of any emergencies."

➤ At ten, relax your hands and forearms, allowing the tension to flow first through your right hand and exit out the fingertips as a brilliant white light flows into its place. Then feel the tension flowing from your left forearm out through the tips of your fingers on the left hand, which is followed by the healing, brilliant white light.

➤ At nine, let the brilliant white light flow into your upper arms, pushing the tensions away as the healing flows into your biceps and triceps. Say to yourself, "I feel good, relaxed, and happy."

➤ At eight, your shoulders and neck are completely relaxed as the brilliant white light of healing bathes them and relaxes the tension.

➤ At seven, the brilliant white light that sits on the crown of your head is glowing as it sends the healing light to all parts of your body. The top of your head, forehead and eyes, cheeks, lips, and jaw are all relaxed and pulsing with the healing energy of the brilliant white light.

➤ At six, you are relaxing more and more as the energy continues to proceed down your body.

➤ At five, your lungs, upper back, and chest are releasing the tension as the brilliant white light flows into to heal and relax you.

➤ At four, your stomach is completely relaxed. There is no tension or discomfort in the area that is filled with the white light of healing. Your lower back is relaxed as the white light pulses through your spine and heals all of the area, releasing the tension.

➤ At three, the muscles in your arms and legs are completely relaxed.

➤ At two, the brilliant white, pulsing light is surrounding your body and moves into your calves, feet, and toes. It exits your body through your toes and comes back up to the top of your head.

➤ At one, you are totally relaxed all over. All of the tension is gone from your body, and the healing white light surrounds you with healing energy and protection. You are calm and happy.

➤ Say to yourself, "I can create any image, creature, or vision I choose. I control my journeys and remember everything in detail that occurs during the experience."

➤ Say to your subconscious mind, "I will say the word 'relax' when I feel my confidence is in jeopardy, and I will immediately gain control of my feelings. I will feel confident in what I am pursuing and will not feel threatened by anyone who is better at the task or quicker. I will perform this task to the best of my ability and feel good about my accomplishment."

➤ Say to your subconscious mind, "I will say relax when I meet someone who threatens my self-confidence. I know I can accomplish anything I choose to pursue over time." (Repeat this with as many statements that are positive about your self-confidence as you need. Remember not to overwhelm your psychic mind.)

➤ When you are ready to return to the present, begin counting from one to ten. Open your eyes, and find yourself completely awake and in your safe place.

Practice #6: Improving the Skills You Choose

➢ Go to your safe practice place where you are free from internal and external distractions. Begin your breathing in and out. Feel the tensions leaving your body as the relaxation takes over.

➢ Close your eyes.

➢ Go to the meadow of time.

➢ You will now bring forth an image of you performing whatever skill you are working on (for example, golfing, dancing, playing the flute, singing, and so forth). Imagine that you have mastered it. You are performing the skill perfectly, and the accomplishment makes you happy.

➢ Continue to observe this performance, which is perfect. Secure this picture in your mind. Say to your subconscious, "I am asking my psychic mind and higher conscious to facilitate my achievement of this request. I will accomplish the level of success that fits my life mission. I will succeed in becoming all that I can be in performing this skill (name the skill)."

➢ When you are ready to return to the present, open your eyes.

➢ Always document in your journal what you have asked for during a practice and the date of the request.

What you have requested will become a reality if it is part of your life mission. Your mind will steer you toward the goal and resources necessary to make it happen. As with everything in the world of the psychic mind, the greater universal power may have other plans for us on our journey, and our request will ultimately look different from what we originally requested. However, most often, you will begin to picture more completely what you want to accomplish and understand how to get there or make something happen. Keep your visual image at the forefront of your mind, and watch for the results. What you want will also probably require learning and practice. Just like when you decided to develop your psychic ability and make the commitment to practice daily, you may need to do the same with the skill you wish to develop.

CHAPTER 13

Past-life Regression

Finally, I want to touch on the subject of past lives. Many people who do professional work involving the mind, body, and spirit believe in reincarnation. It is a belief we live again to contend with the karma left behind from the previous life. Buddhists believe that part of the grief or misfortune we encounter during the current life is the result of actions in the previous life. Each time we work through an uncomfortable event, we are closer to achieving enlightenment. If this is the case, it could be that an individual might never be free from the consequences of their karma, given that everyone will create a negative situation to work through that which perhaps has nothing to do with a debt paid for previous life transgression. However, I believe it is a bit more complex than this explanation. Consider how the intelligence of the universe is involved in all actions related to existence. We are but instruments, channels, conduits, and sources in this world who are here to serve the ultimate intelligence. Each time we enter the physical world, our mission is to gain knowledge that will assist us in becoming enlightened about all things in the universe. Therefore, I believe one is constantly building their karma toward a positive end and not paying for old debts. The intent of our lives then must be to awaken our true self to the extent that is possible each time we complete a life in the physical world.

I was raised in a Christian family among members who would be considered gifted in the psychic field today, given that no one received professional training on the subject. My father and mother were devout in the belief of a higher authority. However, I remember my father approaching the subject of reincarnation with the family on many different occasions. He believed we live several different life times with the goal of advancing our universal intelligence. I never doubted the possibility I may have existed during a different time. While during my childhood I had no personal experiences where I could recall life in another time, many people who interacted with me considered me to be wise beyond my years. However, I did not consider myself to be unusual since information on various subjects seemed to always come to mind without the benefit of study or I would suddenly know where to find an answer. It was during my early teens, after many different experiences with the other side, that I became convinced we live multiple lives.

Religion can inhibit how we choose to approach this subject, so each person must act on what is comfortable for him or her. Because I had the experience of seeing materialized spirits from an early age, the idea that people stayed sleeping in the grave or ascended to heaven forevermore was obviously contradicted by the experience. I believed in God and the Son of God, Jesus Christ. However, I also suspected there was probably more to the story than what I had been taught. As my repertoire of encounters increased, I knew life in the physical world and existence in the spiritual realm was quite complex and full of wondrous possibilities. Finally, I concluded for myself that the spirit is a beautiful creation of light and intelligence. The soul is in and out of the physical body until it achieves a state of perfect knowledge. However, until this state occurs the soul will build on the experiences it has each time it enters a physical body.

What I became curious about was the cycle of repetition in life and how that would influence future lives. Since few spirits, while in the physical body, are free from what one might refer to as sin or transgressions against others, how does this behavior impact the soul's progress? Obviously, each soul born into the physical body will experience the drives of every other creature in the world. I considered the belief that negative karma follows an individual spirit to another life as cruel if there was no opportunity to redeem yourself. Then it occurred to me that since each of us must learn certain lessons in order to progress, there had to be an opportunity to rectify the wrongs we commit in life so that we do not continue to make the same mistake repeatedly.

Consequently, I believe we take our learning into the next life and build upon the experience. Although there are times when the free will of the human can thwart the learning process for the embodied soul, this simply means the soul must return to learn the lessons that were missed. Even if this occurs, there is a reason it happens. So it is important to be mindful of your actions involving others and make every attempt to treat all living creatures in a positive manner. Correcting an indiscretion that causes someone unnecessary pain will result in having learning experiences that assist you in understanding your actions. If the lesson does not come in this life time you will experience it in the next life time.

Everything happens for a reason and each of us plays a role in the life experience.

Now you will have the opportunity to practice past-life regression, if this is something you choose to do as part of your psychic development.

Practice #1: The Timepiece

➤ Go to your place of practice that is free of distractions and find your position. Close your eyes, and allow your whole body to relax. Feel safe as you breathe in healing air and exhale any toxins from the day.

➤ Begin to notice how calm you are feeling and how the deep breaths you are taking in help you to become increasingly relaxed.

➤ Say to your subconscious, "I am relaxing now." You find yourself becoming increasingly more relaxed. Say to yourself, "I am relaxed, free from worry, and alert yet comfortable. I know that my guardian angel will make me aware of any emergencies." You will now begin counting down from ten to one.

➤ At ten, relax your hands and forearms, allowing the tension to flow first through your right hand and exit out the fingertips as a brilliant white light flows into its place. Then feel the tension flowing from your left forearm out through the tips of your fingers on the left hand, which is followed by the healing, brilliant white light.

➤ At nine, let the brilliant white light flow into your upper arms, pushing the tensions away as the healing flows into your biceps and triceps. Say to yourself, "I feel good, relaxed, and happy."

➢ At eight, your shoulders and neck are completely relaxed as the brilliant white light of healing bathes them and relaxes the tension.

➢ At seven, the brilliant white light that sits on the crown of your head is glowing as it sends the healing light to all parts of your body. The top of your head, forehead and eyes, cheeks, lips, and jaw are all relaxed and pulsing with the healing energy of the brilliant white light.

➢ At six, you are relaxing more and more as the energy continues to proceed down your body.

➢ At five, your lungs, upper back, and chest are releasing the tension as the brilliant white light flows in to heal and relax you.

➢ At four, your stomach is completely relaxed. There is no tension or discomfort in the area that is filled with the white light of healing. Your lower back is relaxed as the white light pulses through your spine and heals all of the area, releasing the tension.

➢ At three, the muscles in your arms and legs are completely relaxed.

➢ At two, the brilliant white, pulsing light is surrounding your body and moves into your calves, feet, and toes. It exits your body through your toes and comes back up to the top of your head.

➢ At one, you are totally relaxed all over. All of the tension is gone from your body, and the healing white light surrounds you with healing energy and protection. You are calm and happy.

➢ You are now in the meadow of time. A timepiece hanging in the sky is in front of you. This is your timepiece, and it points out dates and shows the specific time.

➢ Sit on the grass, and watch the hands on the timepiece begin to slowly move backwards. As you watch the hands move backwards, you begin to notice the further back in time they go, the faster they begin to move.

➢ The feeling you are having is so soothing as you watch the hands moving faster and faster. Suddenly, you stop the hands. Observe as the hands on the timepiece begin slowing down. Say to the hands, "Stop!" Stand up and walk under the clock.

➢ Look to your right and to your left. Determine what time it is, day or night. Where are you now? What is your environment like? What do you see?

➢ Take a moment to look at yourself. Are you male or female? What type of clothing are you dressed in? From what period? Do you know your name? If there are people around, move forward to greet them or mingle. Is someone familiar with you? How do you feel? If you choose, continue to gather details for as long as you are comfortable.

➢ When you are ready to return to the present, you will turn and look behind you to see the timepiece. Walk back under the timepiece and then turn to see the hands on the timepiece. Now say, "Return to the present."

➢ You can choose to visit another time just by asking the clock to begin. As the hands begin to turn you will notice they move faster and faster. Once again observe the hands on the timepiece begin to slow. When you are ready say to the hands, "Stop!" Stand up and walk under the clock and repeat the inquiries about yourself, where you are as well as noting the date and time.

➢ You can also choose to go back to the present by turning and walking back under the timepiece and then turn to see the hands on the timepiece. Now say, "Return to the present."

➢ When you return, keep notes in your journal about the experience. Try to remember names, streets, how people were dressed, and any conversations you might have had. Remember to note the date of your travel and what date and time you think you experienced.

In this practice, you can choose to travel into the future, experience parallel universes or realities, and commune with the soul.

Practice #2: Focusing the Experience

➢ Go to your place of practice that is free from distractions, and take your position. Before beginning your relaxation process, imagine where you want to travel. Do you want to travel back in time or forward? Imagine what you will be wearing, and see yourself fully dressed. Remember where you want to go, and say to your subconscious, "When I arrive in the meadow of time and stand before the timepiece, it will take me to the year 2010." (Remember, you will use whatever date is of interest to you. 2010 is only an example.)

➢ Now close your eyes, and allow your whole body to relax. Feel safe as you breathe in healing air and exhale any toxins from the day. The brilliant white light of protection surrounds you and heals as it radiates from your body.

➤ Begin to notice how calm you are feeling and how the deep breaths you are taking helps you to become increasingly relaxed.

➤ Say to your subconscious, "I am relaxing now." You find yourself becoming increasingly more relaxed. Say to yourself, "I am relaxed, free from worry, and alert yet comfortable. I know my guardian angel will make me aware of any emergencies." You will now begin counting down from ten to one.

➤ At ten, relax your hands and forearms, allowing the tension to flow first through your right hand and exit out the fingertips as a brilliant white light flows into its place. Then feel the tension flowing from your left forearm out through the tips of your fingers on the left hand, which is followed by the healing, brilliant white light.

➤ At nine, let the brilliant white light flow into your upper arms, pushing the tensions away as the healing flows into your biceps and triceps. Say to yourself, "I feel good, relaxed, and happy."

➤ At eight, your shoulders and neck are completely relaxed as the brilliant white light of healing bathes them and relaxes the tension.

➤ At seven, the brilliant white light that sits on the crown of your head is glowing as it sends the healing light to all parts of your body. The top of your head, forehead and eyes, cheeks, lips, and jaw are all relaxed and pulsing with the healing energy of the brilliant white light.

➢ At six, relax more and more as the energy continues to proceed down your body.

➢ At five, your lungs, upper back, and chest are releasing the tension as the brilliant white light flows in to heal and relax you.

➢ At four, your stomach is completely relaxed. There is no tension or discomfort in the area that is filled with the white light of healing. Your lower back is relaxed as the white light pulses through your spine and heals all of the area, releasing the tension.

➢ At three, the muscles in your arms and legs are completely relaxed.

➢ At two, the brilliant white, pulsing light is surrounding your body and moves into your calves, feet, and toes. It exits your body through your toes and comes back up to the top of your head.

➢ At one, you are totally relaxed all over. All of the tension is gone from your body, and the healing white light surrounds you with healing energy and protection. You are calm and happy.

➢ You are now in the meadow of time. Before you, suspended in the sky, is a timepiece. This is your timepiece, and it points out dates and shows the specific time.

➢ Sit on the grass, and watch the hands on the timepiece begin slowly moving in the direction of time where you intend to visit. As you watch the hands move, notice they are going faster and faster.

➢ The feeling you are having is so soothing as you watch the hands. Suddenly, the hands begin slowing down and stop at exactly the time and date you have chosen. Stand up and walk under the clock.

> Look to your right and to your left. Determine where you are and what the environment is like. What do you see?

> Take a moment to look at yourself. Are you male or female? What type of clothing are you now wearing? Do you know your name? If there are people around, move forward to greet them or mingle. Is someone familiar to you? How do you feel? If you choose, continue to gather details for as long as you are comfortable.

> When you are ready to return to the present, you will turn and look behind you to see the timepiece. Walk back under the timepiece and then turn to see the hands on the face. You can now choose to return to the present or take another journey.

> You can choose to visit another time just by asking the clock to begin and stating the date and time you want to visit. As the hands begin to turn you will notice they move faster and faster. Once again observe the hands on the timepiece begin to slow. When you are ready say to the hands, "Stop!" Stand up and walk under the clock and repeat the inquiries about yourself, where you are and the date and time.

> You can also choose to go back to the present by turning and walking back under the timepiece and then turn to see the hands on the timepiece. Now say, "Return to the present."

> When you return, make notes in your journal about the experience. Try to remember names, streets, how people were dressed, and any conversations you might have had.

Remember to note the date of your travel and how successful you were in programming the experience.

Past-life regression is multifaceted and quite complex. I have only touched the surface of the fascinating potential this ability, once learned, can afford the individual who wants to explore other times, lives, and dimensions. The subject has been well studied and generally involves a professional hypnotherapist who may use multiple techniques with an individual to help them achieve regression and identify who they were in a previous life. This practice is one more tool you can use as you continue to develop psychic ability.

As a child and throughout my adult life, I would spontaneously experience out-of-body travel, or astral projection. The experience of past-life regression occurred for me later in life. Once again, it came quite naturally. During one of my first experiences, I did not set a time for the timepiece to stop. I allowed the hands to stop when it felt natural. As I walked through the timepiece and into a field, I was looking down at my feet. I saw a boot made of skin that seemed to have a metal toe. My legs were covered with wool leggings, which still makes me itch when I remember the experience. I had a metal hat of sorts under my arm. As I turned my head, a man was beside me. The fellow was talking to me and joking about how many times we had fought together. I can see his dark hair and hear his laugh. I did not respond to the man, but I knew we had a deep connection and friendship. As I looked in front of me, I could see a ridge and heard the snort of a horse behind me. At that moment, I asked to return to the present and walked back through the timepiece into the present time. I cannot say for sure when the clock stopped. However, I sensed it might be between 400 and 1000 BC. I did not see my face, but I knew I was of slender build and young. I had just come from a battle. The experience was so real that I decided to return early.

In another experience, once again, I allowed the timepiece to stop naturally and did not attempt to preprogram my journey. When I walked through the timepiece, I found myself in a small village. I could not understand the language, although I did not feel uncomfortable among the villagers. They noticed me immediately when a young boy came running up to greet me as if I was a parent. I called the child Eimm. As I reached down and bundled him up into my arms, I hugged him tightly. His laugh was strangely familiar, and I felt overwhelmed with great joy as I heard the child. When I put the child down on the ground, I looked at my fingers and realized my fingernails were quite dirty. Then I felt the weight of the heavy skirt I was wearing as I reached down to pick up what appeared to be a basket full of vegetables or fruit. I then asked to return to the time present and turned to walk back through the timepiece. I sensed I had known the spirit of the boy before.

You may not achieve regression during your first attempts, and you should not be discouraged. Practice is the key to mastery, as well as focus. If you should want to explore the subject more deeply, extensive literature is available that will provide you with additional learning and insight.

CHAPTER 14

In Summary

Incorporating you psychic gift into everyday life will now come naturally if you have been faithful in completing your practices. In every aspect of living, just to name a few, you can use what you have learned to help others, direct your own life, or deal with the basic frustrations associated with living in a chaotic world.

By now, you are probably more aware of your surroundings and what is occurring in the physical as well as the spiritual realm. While not everyone will become a professional psychic, you can look for opportunities to use your gift. If I see a person who is experiencing car trouble on the highway, I send a psychic message of love and then bless their car, asking the car to start so they can get to a place that is safe. I also love animals, and their spirits are attracted to me, just like those of humans. I do not hesitate to send a psychic message to deceased animals I encounter and pray for their safe arrival to the spiritual world. There is any number of opportunities to use the gift on a daily basis, and you can take advantage.

When I entered graduate school, I asked my guardian angel to direct me to the information I needed for my research and to assist me in comprehending everything I read. The process was amazing, and, in every instance, my wish was granted. Additionally, I have always used my psychic abilities to locate lost items in the house, in the ivy, and elsewhere. I go to my basic psychic level and ask my guardian angel to direct me to the location or tell me where to go. It then occurs. I use my skills daily and engage in several variations of the practices each day.

As a psychic, you are utilizing a gift that is special because you have developed the skill and are a conduit for the universal intelligence and power. The one, very important issue I touched on previously is remaining humble, remember you are not the source of power associated with your abilities. In no way must your ego enter into this practice, or you might easily lose the capability and privilege of utilizing the gift evermore.

During my childhood, I recognized I had the ability to see, hear, and sense things that most people could not. I quietly acknowledged my gift. When information on the subject of spiritual encounters was discussed, I listened intensely. It was an unspoken law in my family that what we experienced in the psychic and spiritual realm was discussed seriously among family members only. I was aware of the fact that the outside world would not understand or accept my ability. However, something else started to happen as a result of accepting my gift. I developed a sense of freedom from the mainstream of society. I started to appreciate people and nature as unique linkages with a greater existence. At the age of six, I would spend hours beneath two, tall fir trees thinking about how everything interacted and was dependent on something else. The world became increasingly more transparent and it was clear that there was more to our existence than could be imagined. While I participated normally in society, I felt confident and secure in having access to a universe that most ignored.

Just as I did as I grew in my psychic abilities, you will begin to notice more things happening as your psychic mind blends with your conscious self. As a psychic medium, I see flashes of information, pictures, and events that may or may not be connected to a reading. There are times when I look at an individual and see spirits standing near them or receive some piece of information pertaining to their life or even their health. Many things I see are quite difficult to explain according to the parameters of the physical world. You too will have these experiences and become more comfortable with a world that exists out side of the physical realm. There is a quiet confidence you will assume as you have more experiences and confirm your ability.

You will see that all things and people are interconnected, interacting for a short period and then moving on. While some linger and become part of the permanent structure of your life, others come and go. You may find yourself interacting with people different from your previous relationships. Negative or challenging relationships you once related to may gradually disappear from your life as you begin to view the world differently. These experiences you have are in giving and receiving as well as learning and teaching. All will attribute to your greater happiness. The key is to always send positive energy into the universe and never negative. Whatever you give, so shall you receive. The universe responds in kind, so practice shielding yourself from the negative and sending out or thinking only positive thoughts. Always send love, not with the intention of receiving something in return, but from the genuine depth of your heart. If your heart is dark and creates an expectation in return for a kind favor or act, you could very well spoil what you are attempting to do.

When you open your mind and environment to the other side expect the unusual to occur. Prepare yourself for the unknown by acquainting yourself with what can occur during spiritual visitations. One of my favorite encounters involved a group of spirits who had obviously been traveling minstrels. The group announced its arrival in my family room with the blowing of a horn. Then several instruments played in conjunction with singing. I cannot explain this event in a way that does it justice. The music was sharp and distinct. Clearly, it was coming from another dimension, and this group wanted my attention. My husband and I were both amused and startled by the event. Do not be surprised to have such encounters that occur in a flash and leave you wanting more. The other side provides interesting communications most of the time when you are attuned to your higher consciousness.

Another incident that was unusual involved a woman I had read during a session who was persistent in requesting that I attempt to identify her guardian angel. Because of her Native American background, she believed her guardian was an Indian who rode a horse. During the first two attempts to contact her guardian, I saw a drifting energy without form. When I attempted to contact the substance, there was no response. Finally, during a meditation session in the meadow of time, I asked my guardian angel to join me. I then asked for the guardian angel of the woman (who I will refer to as Lea) to come forward. I turned my head to the right as I sat in the meadow with my guardian angel sitting beside me, only to see a very tall creature walking toward me with a large head and very dark eyes. While there appeared to be a mouth, it did not open. The creature identified itself as Lea's guardian angel and gave me its name. The angel stood with me for a while and then let me know they stood at Lea's side at all times. The angel walked out of the meadow and disappeared. This was not a being I had encountered before and I found their appearance to be fascinating.

Aside from your evolution as a psychic and the experiences you will have as with the spiritual realm, remember that the path we take in life is part of our greater mission. Once you have programmed your goals, let your subconscious psychic mind be your guide. I was guided toward using my gift as a medium professionally. I attempted to go in many different directions in life, putting my psychic abilities on the side while I attended college and then established a career as a social worker. Yet, I was constantly brought back on to the path and redirected toward what I was intended to accomplish in life. Listen to the messages that come through for you from your guardians and mentors on the other side. In the end it will serve you well in guiding you toward the correct path.

Everyone is a field of energy existing within a universe of uninterrupted power. We are all moving toward existing in a state of complete knowledge and, ultimately, bonding with the universal source of utmost power (God). By taking the initiative and learning how to use your psychic ability, you now have the basic knowledge and will receive the necessary assistance from the universe to complete your journey, if you choose to do so. That which is available to you is neither evil nor good. It is simply available as energy or power. You are the one who makes the choice on how to use your ability.

Again, remember what you send out into the universe is what will come back to you, so do use caution and good judgment. When you have made a decision and act upon the decision, it becomes yours. There is no turning back. If it is not part of this life plan, chances are you will correct your path during this lifetime or in the next. Whatever is in your consciousness is what is with you at all times. You create your life, the situations in which you live, and the circumstances surrounding your existence. If it is in your consciousness, it will occur, and no one can interfere with the process or outcome. The important thing is to actively listen to the information that comes to you and take action. Every communication and thing you need to know will become increasingly more transparent as you develop your skills. There may be times when you question if anything is actually occurring and it seems there are more obstacles than you had anticipated. Do not be discouraged. Continue on your path. Everything happens for a reason, and the universe as well as your psychic mind are steering the course.

As you sense your growing awareness of what is going on in the world, you will have what you believe to be profound insights. Document them in your journal, along with the other experiences you have during the practices. At this point, listen carefully to your psychic mind as you come to know more and more about our existence on the earth and what life is about. You are a psychic and can access information that cannot be described in ordinary terms. Think about what you feel, hear, see, and who now looks different from when you started the learning.

Your successes will be dependent on the goals you must accomplish this life in order to complete your mission. In addition, each of us plays a role in the life mission of others.

One of the most difficult pieces of our life puzzle is learning what we need to do in life in order to stay on the proper path. There is a force in the intelligent universe greater than ourselves that keeps us directed toward our goal. While each us may explore different opportunities or see ourselves performing great feats that make us heroes, the fact is that our mission may be to simply send love and comfort to someone who is in ill health or hurting emotionally. The kindness they receive for the moment they experience our love or good wishes may be enough to help them through a difficult time or set them free from a burden that was not their own to bear. The point I am trying to make is that we are all connected in this world. For every action, there is an equal or greater reaction. What you might consider small could be the act that influences the life of someone who becomes the next president, and that was what you came to achieve in this life. Nothing in this life happens without purpose or consequence.

For ourselves, if a goal does not turn out exactly as we had intended, the different outcome may be what was supposed to occur for us in reality. While we can sense, predict, and create many things as psychics, we are not all-powerful and do not know all there is to know. A higher universal power is at work and knows what must occur to keep the balance and assist everyone in carrying out his or her life work. Always be kind to yourself, and understand you will not always be right nor will you always be able to help. Remain focused on the positive energy that you emit and continue to do so.

ADDENDUM

Definitions:

➢ Clairaudience: The ability to hear outside of the normal range of hearing. Hearing sounds outside of the normal frequency.

➢ Clairvoyance: The receipt of information through extrasensory perception.

➢ Dowsing: Finding lost articles, objects, or water using a stick or instrument.

➢ Ghost: A spirit or image of a person who is deceased appearing as if alive.

➢ Guardian Angel: An angel who is given the charge or responsibility to protect all living beings from harm and guide us along the path of life. All people have a guardian angel.

➢ Haunted: A place where a spirit is attached and appears repeatedly. In addition, individuals who communicate with the dead such as mediums, channelers, or individuals who hunt ghosts can attract ghosts who attach themselves to the person.

➢ Kinetic Energy: When spirits move objects or things.

➤ Lucid dreams: Guiding what occurs in the dream state.

➤ Materialization: When a spirit temporarily manifests as a physical or smoky form.

➤ Necromancy: Communications with the dead and divining.

➤ Paranormal: Occurrences considered to be outside of the normal range of experiences or scientific explanation.

➤ Premonition: A vague feeling or sense about a future event.

➤ Psychic: A medium or channeler of communications from the spiritual realm.

➤ Psycho kinesis: Mind over matter. The process is often demonstrated through bending dinner flatware.

➤ Psychometry: Through the handling of objects and extrasensory perception, an individual feels the vibrations to identify something about a person or situation.

➤ Sixth Sense: Also known as extrasensory perception (ESP), the ability to send and receive information that incorporates the senses of sight, sound, taste, touch, and smell.

➤ Spirit: The energy that exists within and outside of the physical body, otherwise known as the soul.

➤ Supernatural: Events that have no scientific explanation, often involving apparitions and, in some cases, negative energy materializing to do harm or create fear.

➤ Telekinesis: Involves moving or altering an object through thought.

➤ Telepathy: Communicating from a distance through sending and receiving information.

JOURNAL OF EXPERIENCES

Date: _____

Practice #: _____

Chapter #:_____

Type of practice:_____

I accomplished:

_____

_____

_____

I experienced:

_____

_____

_____

_____

_____

I saw:

_____

_____

_____

_____

_____

I smelled:

_____

_____

_____

_____

_____

I sensed:

_____

_____

_____

_____

_____

I heard:

_____

_____

_____

_____

_____

My environment looked like:

_____

_____

_____

_____

_____

I communicated with:

_____

_____

_____

_____

_____

I was (male or female) and:

_____

_____

_____

_____

_____

I received this message:

_____

_____

_____

_____

General notes regarding the experience:

_____

_____

_____

_____

In Summary

_____

_____

_____

_____

978-0-595-35906-6
0-595-35906-X

9 780595 359066